THE GLE

D1236489

GEOGRAPHY

AND

HISTORY

OF

JAMAICA

FOR USE IN PRIMARY AND
SECONDARY SCHOOLS
and for the
GENERAL READER

The Gleaner Company

Published in Jamaica
by The Gleaner Company Limited
7 North Street, P O Box 40
Kingston, Jamaica, W.I.

© The Gleaner Company *1995*
Twenty-fourth Edition (Revised)
ISBN 976-612-015-3

Printed in Jamaica by: XPRESS LITHO LTD.

FOREWORD

Several generations of children have been taught from the *Gleaner Geography and History of Jamaica,* which has now reached its twenty-third edition. Its earliest function was to supplement the English primers which had been the only schoolbooks available to the Department of Education.

The realization grew that geography and history, more than any other studies, must begin with our own native land. Teachers responded eagerly, and the idea was powerfully aided by the founding of the University of the West Indies.

This handbook has played its part and will continue to do so. But, like all human instruments, it needs to be brought up to date from time to time. It has been improved with each new printing. The present edition takes note of events since Independence and offers revised figures on population, agriculture and natural resources generally. It also presents the National Anthem, the National Prayer, the National Pledge, a National Song for schools, the National Emblems and the National Heroes.

PREFACE

This is the story of a people and the land they live in. It tells how the people came to be here and what they do. It records their progress to freedom. It tells too, something of the land, how it has one of the best climates in the world, how varied and colourful are the history and geography of the island.

Geography is the science which studies the earth as the home of humankind. In our study of the geography of Jamaica, we endeavour to see how human beings in this particular area adapt themselves to their surroundings, and how geographic factors such as world position, climate, soil and rainfall affect their lives.

The study of geography has long since changed from mere memorization of facts and names of places to a logical system of determining cause and effect and of understanding the underlying principles of geography.

It is therefore essential for the student to learn the basic principles of general global, geography while the study of this particular island is undertaken. Elementary factors such as lines of longitude and latitude, structure of the earth, day and night, equinox, land and sea breezes, must be firmly grasped before any regional geography can be fully appreciated.

By examining both the history and the geography of their country, students will discover how the formation of the land has influenced the activities of the people who live there and how those people have shaped the land to suit their own purposes.

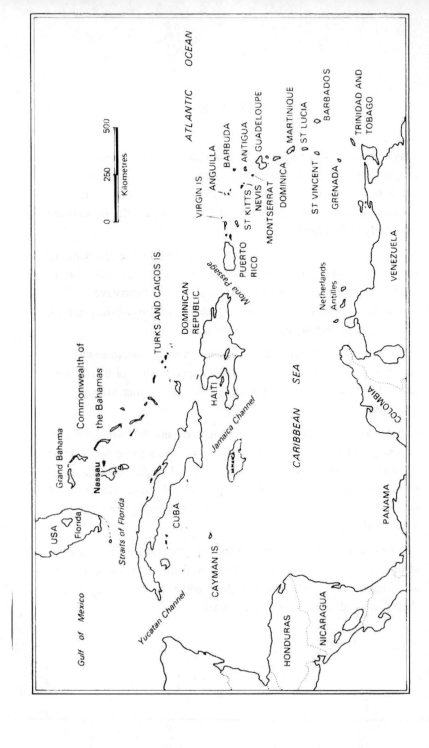

CONTENTS

ILLUSTRATIONS

INTRODUCTION

National Heroes and Symbols of Nationhood

In 1969, the Parliament of Jamaica adopted a resolution establishing formally the **Order of the National Hero,** Jamaica's highest honour. It is awarded for most distinguished service to the nation. The motto of the Order is "He built a city which hath foundation".

Marcus Garvey (1887-1940) was declared a National Hero in 1964 when his body, which had been interred in a London cemetery since 1940, was reclaimed by the Jamaican Government and entombed at National Heroes Park. The National Heroes Bill, which was passed in 1969, gave retroactive Parliamentary authority to his declaration as Jamaica's first National Hero in 1964. Marcus Garvey brought pride to the disadvantaged black peoples of Jamaica, the USA and the world. He preached equality and proposed means to achieve it.

The 1969 National Heroes Bill also gave retroactive authority to the declaration in 1965 of two other National Heroes: **Paul Bogle** (c.1825-1865) and **George William Gordon** (1822-1865)

Paul Bogle and George William Gordon were declared National Heroes during the 1965 observance of the Centenary of the 1865 Morant Bay Rebellion, when they were put to death on the authority of Governor Eyre. They had led the people in their struggle against poverty and the government's denial of their rights.

In September 1969, **Norman Manley** (1893-1969) and **Alexander Bustamante** (1884-1977), the twin creators of Independent Jamaica, were declared National Heroes on the recommendation of a National Committee. They had founded the two-party political system which has been the centre-piece of Jamaica's democratic political development and they led Jamaica into Independence in 1962. The Right Excellent Norman Manley had died in early September 1969, so the Right Excellent Alexander Bustamante became the only National Hero to be so declared in his lifetime.

Two more National Heroes were named in 1975. They were **Sam Sharpe** (1780-1833), the leader of a historic slave revolt in 1832, and **Nanny,** the sister of Cudjoe, the famous Maroon leader. Nanny was

JAMAICAN CURRENCY

Our Jamaican coins and bank notes reflect our pride in our National Heroes and other notable Jamaicans

Twenty Dollars: a bi-metallic coin, outer ring nickel-brass, inner core cupro-nickel. The Right Excellent Marcus Mosiah Garvey is featured.

Ten Dollars: twelve scalloped nickel-plated steel. The Right Excellent George William Gordon is featured.

Five Dollars: a round, milled coin with eight lobes within the circle and a silver finish. The Right Excellent Norman Manley is featured.

One Dollar: a seven-sided, plain-edged coin, with a silver finish. The Right Excellent Sir Alexander Bustamante is featured.

Twenty-five cents: a round, plain-edged copper coloured coin. The Right Excellent Marcus Garvey is featured.

Ten cents: a round, plain-edged, copper coloured coin. The Right Excellent Paul Bogle is featured.

$500 Nanny of the Maroons

$100 Sir Donald Sangster

$50 Sam Sharpe

$1000 Michael Manley

the undefeated leader of the Maroons in Portland and a town in the Blue Mountains was renamed Nanny Town in her honour. Parliamentary approval was given in March 1982.

The National Heroes are referred to as "The Right Excellent".

Each of the National Heroes is associated with one of the fourteen parishes of Jamaica:

Marcus Garvey with **St. Ann**. He was born and grew up in St. Ann's Bay and a statue to him stands outside St Ann's Bay Library.

Paul Bogle with **St. Thomas**, where he was a Church Deacon. He was hanged in Morant Bay in 1865 and a statue to him stands outside the Court House there.

George William Gordon with **St. Andrew**. He pursued his career as a lawyer in Kingston and his home in Cherry Gardens is a national monument. He too was hanged in Morant Bay in 1865.

Norman Manley with **Manchester**. He was born and grew up in Roxborough

Alexander Bustamante with **Hanover**. He was born in Blenheim and grew up there.

Nanny with **Portland** and especially Nanny Town.

Sam Sharpe with **St. James**. He was a slave there, led his revolt from there and was executed in Montego Bay.

NATIONAL EMBLEMS – The Symbols of Independence

The Flag: A gold Saltire Cross against green and black triangles: "Hardships there are, but the land is green and the sun shineth" .

The National Flower : The Lignum Vitae - a delicate blue flower.

The National Tree :   The Blue Mahoe

The National Bird: The Doctor Bird or Swallow-tail Humming Bird which lives only in Jamaica.

The National Fruit: The Ackee

OUR NATIONAL ANTHEM

Eternal Father bless our land,
Guard us with Thy mighty hand;
Keep us free from evil powers
Be our light through countless hours.
To our leaders, Great Defender,
Grant true wisdom from above.
Justice, Truth be ours forever,
Jamaica, land we love,
Jamaica, Jamaica, Jamaica, land we love.

Teach us true respect for all,
Stir response to duty's call;
Strengthen us the weak to cherish,
Give us vision lest we perish.
Knowledge send us, heavenly Father,
Grant true wisdom from above.
Justice, Truth be ours forever,
Jamaica, land we love,
Jamaica, Jamaica, Jamaica, land we love.

Note. The words of the National Anthem were written by the Hon. the Rev. Dr. Hugh Sherlock, the Founder of Boys' Town. The Hon. Robert Lightbourne, then Minister of Trade and Industry, wrote the music and musician Mapletoft Poole and his wife harmonized the words with the music to create the Anthem approved by Parliament in 1962.

NATIONAL PRAYER

For use weekly in schools.
The Response is; "We give Thee thanks, O God"

Let us Pray: Let us give thanks for all God's goodness and the wonderful heritage into which we have entered; for Jamaica, our island home, the land of our birth —

We give Thee thanks, O God.

For the majesty of our hills, the beauty of our valleys and the flaming loveliness of our gardens —

We give Thee thanks, O God.

For the warmth and brightness of our days and the calm and peace of our countryside —

We give Thee thanks, O God.

For the rich heritage of our people coming from many races, and yet one in purpose, in achievement, and in destiny, and for the dignity of labour and the service given by every citizen of our land.—

We give Thee thanks, O God.

For freedom, just laws and our democratic way of life.—

We give Thee thanks, O God.

For the high privilege and responsibility of Independence and for bringing us to nationhood.—

We give Thee thanks, O God

For our parents, teachers, religious and other leaders and all those who in every walk of life are helping to prepare us for responsible citizenship, and for all those who are giving voluntary service in the public interest.—

We give Thee thanks, O God.

For the poets, artists and thinkers and all who create in us the vision of a new and better society.—

We give Thee thanks, O God.

For our godly heritage, the example of Jesus Christ and the sacrifices of our fathers in the faith.—

We give Thee thanks, O God.

The response to the following is: *"Hear us, we beseech Thee, O God*

Bless, we pray Thee, our Queen, our Governor General, our Prime Minister and other Ministers of State, our Parliament, and all who are set in authority over us and grant that under them we may be peaceful and justly governed.—

Hear us, we beseech Thee, O God

Grant us love and compassion for all those in need and distress and help us to remove poverty and ignorance form our land, and grant us prosperity and true wisdom, we pray.—

Hear us, we beseech Thee, O God

Forgive us all that is unworthy and evil in our national life, establish us in righteousness and inspire us to work for universal brotherhood, we pray.—

Hear us, we beseech Thee, O God

Guide and bless our nation, we pray, and make us loyal and dutiful citizens through Jesus Christ, our Lord, Amen.

THE NATIONAL PLEDGE

For use in schools at the
beginning and end of term and on other special occasions

Before God and all mankind, I pledge the love and loyalty of my heart, the wisdom and courage of my mind, the strength and vigour of my body in the service of my fellow citizens.

I promise to stand up for Justice, Brotherhood and Peace, to work diligently and creatively, to think generously and honestly, so that Jamaica may, under God, increase in beauty, fellowship and prosperity, and play her part in advancing the welfare of the whole human race.

A NATIONAL SONG
For use in schools

I PLEDGE MY HEART

(to the tune of "I Vow to Thee, My Country")

I pledge my heart forever
To serve with humbled pride
This shining homeland ever
So long as earth abide

I pledge my heart this island,
As God and faith shall live.
My work, my strength, my love and
My loyalty to give.
O green isle of the Indies,
Jamaica, strong and free,
Our vows and loyal promises,
O heartland, 'tis to thee!

— by Victor Stafford Reid

The Jamaican Coat of Arms

The Coat of Arms of Independent Jamaica is based on the one
granted to Jamaica in 1661.
In 1962, a new Motto, Out of Many, One People, was chosen
for the Scroll under the Shield.
A male and female Arawak stand on either side of the shield,
representing the original inhabitants.
The Red Cross is a reminder of the association with England.
The five Pineapples represent the Jamaican tradition of hospitality.
The Crest is a Jamaican crocodile surmounting
a Helmet and Mantlings.

SECTION 1: GEOGRAPHY OF JAMAICA

CHAPTER 1

GENERAL DESCRIPTION

Situation and Size

On the map, the islands of the Caribbean look like stepping stones stretching in an arc from the western end of Venezuela in South America to the peninsula of Florida in North America.

The Caribbean islands are divided into two groups: the Greater Antilles and the Lesser Antilles. Forming the northern part of the arc are four large islands, Cuba, Hispaniola (made up of Haiti and the Dominican Republic), Jamaica and Puerto Rico. These are the Greater Antilles. The eastern end of the arc consists of the smaller islands which together form the Lesser Antilles. These include St. Kitts, Nevis, Anguilla, Antigua and Montserrat (this group is called the Leeward Islands), Grenada, St. Lucia, St. Vincent, and Dominica (this group is called the Windward Islands), Barbados, Trinidad and Tobago and the French islands of Martinique and Guadeloupe. The islands vary widely in size, ranging from Cuba and Hispaniola, by far the largest, to the tiny islands of the Grenadines. Those which have English as their official language and are members of the Commonwealth are usually referred to as the **West Indies.**

The body of water bounded by these islands, the northern coast of South America and the Central American isthmus is the Caribbean Sea.

Almost at the centre of the Caribbean Sea, Jamaica lies 150 kilometres (90 miles) south of Cuba and 160 kilometres (100 miles) west of Haiti, the two nearest countries. The closest point to Jamaica in South America is Cartagena in Colombia, a distance of 710 kilometres (445 miles) almost due south. Kingston, the capital of Jamaica, lies approximately 18°N latitude and 78°W longitude.

Jamaica is the largest of the West Indian islands (English-speaking). It has an area of 11,424 square kilometres (4,411 square miles), more than twice the area of Trinidad which is next in size. Jamaica measures 243 kilometres (146 miles) from east to west. Its greatest width is 80 kilometres (51 miles), from St. Ann's Bay to Portland Point. The distance from Kingston to the nearest point on the north coast, Annotto Bay, is 36 kilometers (22 miles).

Jamaica is centrally situated in the Caribbean Zone. It lies on the direct sea routes from the United States of America and Europe to the Panama Canal.

Origin of the Island

Jamaica belongs to the Central American region of the Western Hemisphere. The Caribbean islands are actually the summits of a submarine range of mountains which in prehistoric times perhaps formed one large land mass connecting Central America to Venezuela in South America.

During the ages, vast changes took place in this region of the earth's crust. The land subsided beneath the sea. When it rose again, only the highest parts appeared above the surface of the sea. These formed the Caribbean Islands, which have remained separate and distinct islands ever since.

A close examination of the structure of the islands shows that there is a single mountain range in Puerto Rico which may be regarded as the centre of the submarine system. This range runs into Haiti, where it divides into three separate branches, connected by submarine ridges. The northern branch passes through the north of Cuba as the Organos Mountains, and then into the Peninsula of Yucatan. The central branch passes into southern Cuba as the Sierra Maestra and continues under the sea into Central America. The southern range passes through Jamaica, forming the Blue Mountains, the central mountain range of the island, and continues into Honduras.

East of Puerto Rico the main chain divides itself, forming an inner chain and an outer chain of islands. The inner chain includes St. Lucia, St. Vincent and Grenada. The other chain can be traced through the Virgin Islands, Antigua, Barbados, Tobago and northern Trinidad, continuing into the South American Continent as the coastal mountains of Venezuela.

Description

As Christopher Columbus first set eyes on Jamaica while his fleet steered for what is now St. Ann's Bay on his second voyage of discovery to the New World in 1494, the following thoughts came to him. They are communicated to us by the Spanish historian Andres Bernaldez in the following description:

> It is the fairest island eyes have beheld; mountainous and the land seems to touch the sky; very large; bigger than Sicily, has a circumference of 800 leagues (I mean miles), and all full of valleys and fields and plains; it is very strong and extraordinarily populous; even on the edge of the sea as well as inland it is full of very big villages, very near together, about four leagues apart.

Bernaldez, of course, grossly exaggerated the circumference of the island, which is about 765 kilometres (460 miles); and our mountains do not seem to touch the sky. But although the face of the island has been changed to some degree since then, particularly by the work of man, this description of the island's natural beauty is not unjustified today.

The student of geography will find, nevertheless, that when temperature, soil, vegetation, structure and natural resources are taken into consideration, this semi-tropical island is, from a purely geographical standpoint, an excellent habitation for human beings.

Exercises on Chapter 1

1) Into how many groups are the West Indian islands divided? Name them. To which group does Jamaica belong?

2) What is the length of Jamaica? What is its greatest width? What is area of the island? How far is Cuba from Jamaica?

3) What is the position of the island in terms of latitude and longitude? How is the island situated in terms of the Caribbean? List the advantages which accrue from its position.

4) Was Jamaica always a separate island? How were the Greater Antilles separated from one another?

5) Why is Jamaica described as a semi-tropical island?

6) Which islands form (a) the Windward Islands (b) the Leeward Islands?

CHAPTER 2

PHYSICAL FEATURES

The island of Jamaica can be divided into three main types of land forms: 1) the central mountain chain formed by igneous and metamorphic rocks; 2) the karst limestone hills in the Cockpit area; 3) the low-lying coastal plains and interior valleys. Limestone formations occur all over the island, but especially in the western areas.

Mountains

The most striking physical feature of Jamaica is its mountainous nature. Nearly half the island is over 300 metres (1,000 ft) above sea-level.

The central chain of mountains runs east to west, forming a backbone through the middle of the island. From the central range other ranges run north and south; and from these ridges subordinate spurs branch off in every direction until nearly the whole surface of the island is cut up into ridges and valleys.

The mountain system may be divided into three parts:

1) The eastern section, composed of the Blue Mountains and the John Crow Mountains.

2) The central region, formed chiefly of limestone, extending from Stony Hill to the Cockpit Country.

3) The western section with Dolphin Head as its centre.

THE MAJOR RANGES

The Eastern Section

The Blue Mountains run for about 75 kilometres (44 miles) through the county of Surrey and a part of Middlesex. These are the highest mountains in Jamaica, reaching 2,250 metres (7,402 feet) at Blue Mountain Peak. Subordinate ridges run north and south from the main ridge.

On the south there are the Port Royal mountains, a complicated series of ridges, which run south from Catherine's Peak (1537 metres, 5,056 feet) towards the sea near Albion in St. Thomas. The Queensbury Ridge, starting from Blue Mountain Peak, separates the valley of the Negro River from that of the Yallahs.

Three great ridges branch off to the north. The first branches off from Blue Mountain Peak toward the sea near St. Margaret's Bay in Portland, separating the valley of the Rio Grande from that of the Swift River. The second starts from Silver Hill near Catherine's Peak and forms the watershed between the Buff Bay River and the Spanish River. The third is an extremely high ridge starting from Fox's Gap the boundary of St. Mary and Portland and sending out several spurs which reach the sea between Buff Bay and Annotto Bay.

The   Mountains are the most easterly mountains of Jamaica. They run from the north-west to the south-east in the parish of Portland, and divide the Rio Grande valley from the east coast of the island.

The Central Region

This region begins west of Stony Hill (400 metres/1,361 feet) where the main road to the north crosses the mountains and stretches westwards till it merges into the Cockpit Country. It divides into two parts. One, chiefly of limestone formation, extends west through the Mammee Hill and the Red Hills ending at Bog Walk. The other runs in a north-easterly direction forming the boundary line between St. Mary and St. Catherine. Passing through Guy's Hill, it continues as a well-defined range to Mount Diablo. It then becomes irregular and broken, finally merging with the Cockpit Country.

The Cockpit Country of south Trelawny and parts of St. Elizabeth and St. James is a region of broken elevations and depressions. It is peculiarly wild in character. Formed of white limestone, jagged and irregular, it is dissected by deep sink holes and steep-sided circular arenas. These are formed because rain water dissolves the limestone along cracks in the rocks.

The Western Section

These mountains extend through Westmoreland and Hanover, reaching a height of 1,809 feet at Birch's Hill. Dolphin Head, so called because of its appearance, is a landmark seen from far out at sea to the south.

Other Important Mountains

The Don Figueroa, the May Day and Carpenter Mountains pass through the parish of Manchester lying roughly in an arc north-west to southeast.

The mountains of St. Catherine, to the north of Spanish Town, are a continuation of the Red Hills system of St. Andrew, through which the Rio Cobre has cut its gorge. They are called the St. John, the St. Dorothy and the Guy's Hill Mountains. The Hellshire Hills, to the extreme south of St. Catherine, are an independent group of limestone hills. The Pedro and Dry Harbour Mountains are in the parish of St. Ann. The Mocho Range and the Bull Head Mountains are in the parish of Clarendon. They are both independent mountain ranges. Bull Head Mountain marks the centre of the island.

SOME HIGH MOUNTAIN PEAKS AND PASSES

Parishes	Mountains and Passes	Height	
		Metres	Feet
In St. Thomas	Blue Mountain Peak	2,250	7,402
	Mossman's Peak	2,036	6,700
In Portland	Sugar Loaf Peak	2,128	7,000
	John Crow Mountains, highest point	1,140	3,750
In St. Andrew	Sir John's Peak	1,925	6,332
	Catherine's Peak	1,537	5,056
	Silver Hill Gap	1,067	3,513

		Metres	*Feet*
	Hardwar Gap	1,216	4,000
	Newcastle Parade Ground	1,125	3,702
	Stony Hill, where main road crosses	400	1,361
In St. Catherine	Juan de Bolas Mountain	833	2,743
	Guy's Hill	638	2,100
	Mount Diablo, Hollymount	837	2,754
	Mount Diablo, where main road crosses	547	1,800
In St. Ann	Albion	839	2,759
In Clarendon	Bull Head	845	2,782
In Manchester	Coleyville, Mount Denham	984	3,236
	Mandeville Court House	626	2,060
In St. Elizabeth	Munro College	778	2,560
In Hanover	Dolphin Head	544	1,789

Rivers

Since the principal range of mountains runs from west to east, the rivers, which start on their slopes, generally flow north or south.

Most of the rivers in Jamaica are not navigable. The height of the mountains causes them to run swiftly in deep beds, and their courses are sometimes broken by waterfalls. One exception is the Black River, the longest navigable river in Jamaica. It is 73 kilometres (44 miles) long and for 28 kilometres (17 miles) from its mouth it is navigable by small vessels.

The rivers of Portland, which have their source in the Blue Mountains, flow very swiftly, and can be very destructive in time of heavy rainfall. The Rio Grande, rising on the northern slopes of the Blue Mountains, is a large river which has its course through some of the wildest and most beautiful scenery in the island. Rafting on this river has become, in recent years, a popular sporting pastime and tourist attraction. Other main rivers of Portland are the Swift, Spanish, and Buff Bay.

The Wag Water (formerly Agua Alta) rises in the mountains of St. Andrew and flows through the parish of St. Mary, entering the sea west of Annotto Bay. The Hope River rises in the hills near Newcastle and enters the sea about ten kilometres (6 miles) east of Kingston. Both the Wag Water and the Hope river supply Kingston with water.

The Milk River, which is navigable for some ten kilometres, supplies a system of canals for the irrigation of the plains of Vere in Clarendon. Rising at Windsor in the interior of Trelawny, the Martha Brae discharges into the sea east of Falmouth. The chief river of Westmoreland, the Cabaritta, waters the alluvial district of the area.

With its tributaries rising in the Above Rocks district in St. Andrew, the Rio Cobre runs through St. Catherine. It provides water for drinking and irrigation and is one of the chief sources of water for Kingston and St. Andrew. The Plantain Garden River in St. Thomas is the only important river which does not follow the general rule of rivers flowing north or south. Flowing south in its upper course, it turns east upon meeting the coastal range of hills. It then flows through the fertile Plantain Garden River Valley and enters the sea at Holland Bay.

Special mention must be made of the underground rivers in the limestone region. The Cave and Hectors Rivers are notable examples. The porous nature of the limestone accounts for the scarcity of surface water in the central districts. The parish of St. Ann, because it is chiefly of limestone formation, has no rivers in its interior. When swollen by exceptional rainfall, the underground reservoirs sometimes rise to the surface as lakes. The Moneague Lake near Moneague is a good example of these temporary lakes, remaining above ground sometimes for years.

PRINCIPAL RIVERS

Parishes	Main Rivers
In St. Thomas	The Plantain Garden River, The Yallahs and Morant Rivers.
In Portland	The Rio Grande, The Swift, Buff Bay and Spanish Rivers

In St. Andrew	The Hope and Cane Rivers
In St. Catherine	The Rio Cobre and Ferry Rivers.
In St. Mary	The Wag Water, The Dry River, Rio Nuevo and the White River. (The White River forms the boundary between St. Mary and St. Ann).
In St. Ann	The Roaring River, the Llandovery River and the Rio Bueno between Trelawny and St. Ann.
Between St. Ann & Clarendon	The Cave River.
In Clarendon	The Milk River and Rio Minho.
In St. Elizabeth	The Black River.
In Trelawny	The Martha Brae River.
In St. James	The Great River which divides St. James from Hanover and Westmoreland.
In Westmoreland	The Cabaritta River.

Plains

The plains of Jamaica lie chiefly on the southern side of the island, and are all of alluvial formation. This means that they were formed over the ages by deposits carried by rivers.

The principal plains are the Liguanea Plain in Kingston and St. Andrew, the Rio Cobre and St. Dorothy Plains in St. Catherine, the Plain of Vere in Clarendon, the Pedro Plain in St. Elizabeth, and the George's Plain in Westmoreland.

The valleys of the Morant and Yallahs Rivers, and the Plantain Garden River Valley in St. Thomas, are fertile, low-lying areas formed chiefly of alluvium deposited by the rivers.

Harbours

Kingston Harbour, the seventh largest natural harbour in the world, contains about 13 kilometres (eight miles) of navigable water. It is almost completely landlocked by the Palisadoes, the narrow strip of land which ends at Port Royal, leaving a deep channel through which even the largest ships can sail. During the wars of the seventeenth and eighteenth centuries, all the British naval ships stationed in the West Indies could anchor inside the harbour. Modern developments have made Kingston Harbour an excellent port for shipping of all kinds, capable of accommodating the largest container vessels.

In 1962 a gigantic dredging operation was commenced on the west Kingston shoreline, as a result of which some 750 hectares (300 acres) of land were reclaimed from the sea. On this land, called Newport West, a berthing and cargo-storing complex was established. A similar dredging operation to create Newport East was also completed, 283 hectares of land having been reclaimed. All shipping is now concentrated at these locations which together are known as Port Bustamante. This modern complex replaced the fourteen finger wharves which used to run out into the harbour from the Kingston waterfront.

Port Antonio, on the north coast, with its twin harbours, was once Jamaica's second port, as Montego Bay's open harbour was seen as being too exposed to "northers" (strong winds blowing from the north). Now an extensive deep water harbour has been built in the vicinity of the Bogue islands near the Montego Bay shore, and is in use with three berths available. The area is named Freeport.

Ocho Rios and Port Rhoades on the north and Port Kaiser and Port Esquivel on the south are important ports from which bauxite and alumina are exported. Ocho Rios is also an important port for cruise ships bringing visitors. Other important harbours are Lucea, St. Ann's Bay, Oracabessa and Port Maria on the north, and Morant Bay, Salt River and Black River on the south coast. Runaway Bay and Discovery Bay are mainly of historical interest.

Cays

Several small islands, called cays, lie at various points off the coast of Jamaica. The most important of these are the Morant Cays and the

Pedro Cays. The Morant Cays, four in number, lie on a crescent-shaped shoal 55 kilometres (33 miles) south-east of Morant Point. The Pedro Cays, also four in number, are situated on the Pedro Bank about 66 kilometres (40 miles) south of Portland Point. The Port Royal Cays lie outside Kingston Harbour.

MINERAL SPRINGS

Mineral springs are to be found in Jamaica, some of them of high therapeutic value. The most important are the warm saline and radioactive spring at Milk River in Clarendon, the hot, sulphurous spring at Bath St. Thomas, the Black River Spa in St. Elizabeth and the Moffat Spring on the White River. There are also mineral baths fed by cold springs at Rockfort, near Kingston, and at Port Henderson in St. Catherine.

Exercises on Chapter 2

1) Into what three divisions may the mountain system of Jamaica be divided? What is the most easterly range? Through what parishes do the Blue Mountains run? Where are the Port Royal Mountains? Trace on the map the three northern ridges of the Blue Mountains.

2) Draw a sketch map of Jamaica. Trace on your map the three northern ridges of the Blue Mountains. Trace the central chain which begins west of Stony Hill. What is the highest point in the westerly range?

3) Where is the Cockpit Country? Account for the irregular and broken topography of the Cockpit Counry.

4) Where are the Hellshire Hills? In what parish is the Mocho Range? Of what formation are the mountains of St. Ann?

5) Why are the rivers of Jamaica not an important means of transportation? What is the general direction of the flow of the rivers? What important river is the exception to this rule?

6) Where is the largest river in Jamaica? How long is it? Where is the Rio Grande? Describe the course of the Plantain Garden River. Why does St. Ann have no rivers in its interior?

7) Where are the plains of Jamaica situated? Of what formation are they? In what parish is the George's Plain? Where is the Plain of Vere?

8) Describe Kingston Harbour. Which was once the second port in the island? Describe its harbour.

9) What are the most important cays off Jamaica? Where are they situated?

10) What kind of mineral spring is at Milk River? Name the locations of the mineral springs in the island.

CHAPTER 3

CLIMATE

Climate is the average state of the weather. Weather is concerned with daily changes in temperature, wind, cloud and rain — in general the state of the atmosphere. For instance, one day may be sunny and hot another may be chilly and yet another very rainy. That is the daily weather. But, *generally,* Jamaica is hot and sunny. That is the **climate.**

When we examine Jamaica's climate we are chiefly concerned with

1) Temperature (degree of heat and cold)

2) Winds (their movement and direction)

3) Rainfall (its causes and its seasons).

Temperature

How hot or cold a place is depends mainly on how far it is north or south of the equator. The higher the latitude the colder the climate. What is the latitude of Jamaica? If you look at the globe you will see that Jamaica is in the tropical zone south of the Tropic of Cancer. However, its distance north of the equator has a moderating effect on its temperature, and therefore Jamaica is said to have a semi-tropical climate.

Apart from latitude, the greatest factor in determining the temperature of a country is altitude. Most of the effective heat we enjoy is radiated from the earth which has first been warmed by the sun. To reach the surface of the earth, the sun's rays have to pass through layers of atmosphere, a process which causes it to lose some of its heat. If we imagine these layers of atmosphere as blankets retaining the heat radiated by the earth's surface we will see that by climbing above these layers it will become colder. Temperature decreases by $1.7°$ Celsius (or $1°$ Fahrenheit) for every 100 metres (300 ft) of ascent.

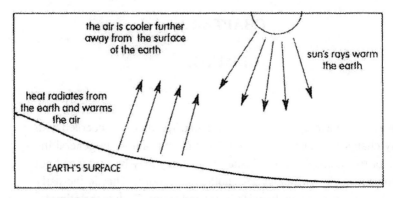

The air temperature falls further away from the earth's surface

Because Jamaica is a very mountainous country, temperatures vary widely in different parts of the island. For example, the temperature might drop to about 10°C or 50°F in Mandeville (626 metres, 2,061 feet above sea level), while in Kingston the mean temperature is 26°C or 78°F. On the whole, Jamaica's temperature has no extremes, especially since the surrounding sea has a moderating effect on the weather, and the variety of climate is considered healthy and beneficial.

Winds

Local winds which blow from the sea on to the land by day and from the land out to sea at night, are very noticeable in Jamaica because it is an island.

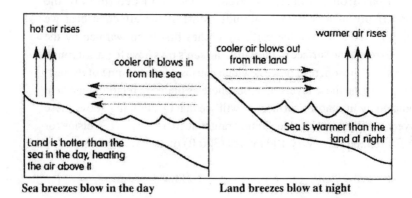

Sea breezes blow in the day   **Land breezes blow at night**

The prevailing winds in the Caribbean are from the north-east. Remember that warm air is lighter than cold and warm air rises. Also winds blow from an area of high pressure to an area of low pressure. At the equator, the hotter air is continually rising, creating an area of low pressure. The air on both sides of the equator, being cooler and heavier, moves in to take the place of the rising air, hence there is a constant movement of air towards the equator, from the north and south. However, since the earth turns from west to east, the winds do not blow due south or north, but are slightly deflected (turned) so that they come from a north-east direction north of the equator, and from a south-east direction south of the equator.

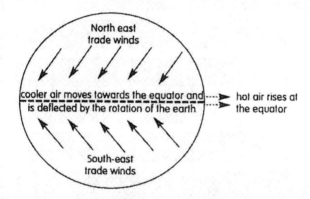

Winds move from the north-east north of the equator and from the south-east south of the equator.

These movements of air around the equator are called the Trade Winds. Since they blow from a cooler to a warmer part of the earth, they are able to hold more moisture, and so bring rainfall.

Rainfall

The heat of the sun acts like the fire under a kettle and turns water from the various water bodies of the world into water vapour. This process is called **evaporation.** If the temperature of air is lowered, the water vapour it contains in the form of clouds will fall as rain. This process is called **condensation.**

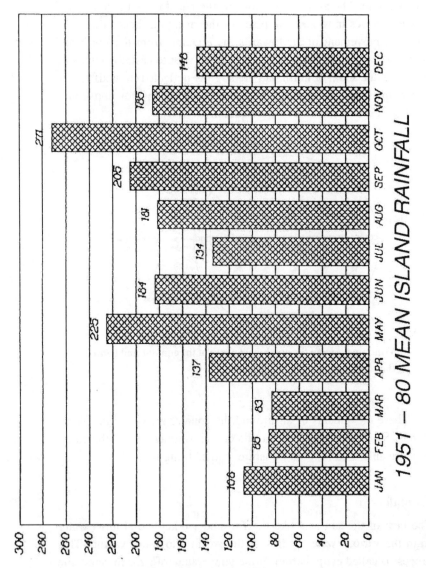

1951 – 80 MEAN ISLAND RAINFALL

Jamaica receives two kinds of rainfall: convectional and relief.

Moisture-laden air may be cooled and thus forced to give up its water vapour in the form of rain in two ways. In both cases, condensation takes place and rain falls.

In the first case, when evaporation takes place, the moist air rises. As it rises it cools and condensation takes place causing rain. Rains originating in this way are known as *convectional rains.*

In the second case, when the moisture-bearing trade winds come upon a high mountain range, they are forced to rise; the air cools and condensation takes place, and the rain which results is known as *relief rainfall* because it is caused by a change in altitude. The air deposits its moisture as it rises on the windward side of the mountains, and then descends as a dry wind on the leeward side. This dry area is known as the rain shadow.

Relief rainfall causes Port Antonio on the windward side of the Blue Mountains to receive an average of 43 centimetres (17 inches) of rain in November while Kingston, in the rain shadow, receives only 17.5 centimetres (7 inches). Antigua and Barbados, which are two relatively flat, low-lying islands, have a lower rainfall than other more mountainous Caribbean islands.

As a rule, rainfall is much heavier on the North Coast of Jamaica than on the South Coast. The North Coast receives the relief rainfall deposited on the mountains running from west to east, while the South Coast, receives chiefly convectional rain.

Jamaica has two rainy seasons, the first in May and the other in October and November. As a rule, rain follows the sun. It appears to pass over all places between the Tropics of Cancer and Capricorn twice a year. In Jamaica the sun is directly overhead about the second week in May and in early August. Notice that the periods of heavy rainfall reach their maximum shortly after the sun has been directly overhead.

Hurricanes

A hurricane is a storm revolving around a centre of low pressure which contains almost no wind. As a hurricane develops, the winds from the area of high pressure rush in a spiral pattern towards the low-pressure centre, and as their centrifugal force (circular speed) intensifies, powerful gales of up to 200 kilometres (120 miles) per hour are built up. The calm vortex in the centre, the "eye" of the hurricane, varies in diameter from thirty to a few hundred miles, and usually moves westwards. Hurricanes are invariably accompanied by driving rains.

Nowadays weather stations discover hurricanes as soon as they develop and give warning to those places towards where a hurricane may be heading. On the approach of a hurricane the barometer falls and the thermometer usually rises.

The hurricane season is usually between July and October, though a hurricane may occasionally arise in June or November. On September 12, 1988, Jamaica suffered its worst hurricane in living memory when Hurricane Gilbert devastated the island.

Exercises on Chapter 3

1) What are the two main factors which determine the temperature of a country? Explain why temperature falls as altitude increases. At what rate does temperature fall as one goes higher?

2) If you have a thermometer at your school, make a temperature chart and note the highest and lowest changes in temperature. Record on the chart the days on which rain falls.

3) Why is there a movement of air towards the equator? Account for the north-east and south-east direction of the trade winds. Draw a map showing the wind belts of the world.

4) Explain the terms evaporation and condensation. Why does air give up its moisture when it is cooled? Explain relief rain and convectional rain. Distinguish between the windward and leeward side of a mountain.

5) Explain why Portland is the rainiest parish in the island. Why does the north coast of Jamaica enjoy a higher rainfall than the south coast? Account for Jamaica's having two rainy seasons.

6) What is a hurricane? What is the "eye" of a hurricane? How can we tell when a hurricane is approaching?

CHAPTER 4

POLITICAL GEOGRAPHY

(Population figures are taken from the April 7, 1991 census as set out in the Revised Preliminary Figures put out by the office of the Statistical Institute)

Jamaica is divided into three counties: Surrey (2,124 sq. km [820 sq. miles]; Middlesex (5,248 sq. km [2,026 sq. miles]; and Cornwall (4,053 sq. km [1,565 sq. miles]). Surrey is the eastern county, Middlesex the middle county and Cornwall the western county.

The counties are divided into fourteen parishes. Surrey has four parishes: Kingston (including Port Royal), St. Andrew, St. Thomas and Portland. Middlesex has five parishes: St. Catherine, St. Mary, Clarendon, St. Ann and Manchester. Cornwall has five parishes: St. Elizabeth, Trelawny, St. James, Hanover and Westmoreland.

According to the Revised Preliminary Figures from the Statistical Institute of Jamaica, the Population of Jamaica numbered 2,391,273 on April 7, 1991.

Parishes of Surrey

KINGSTON

The parish of Kingston covers an area of over 25 sq. km (10 sq. miles) and a population of 103,404. It is the capital of Jamaica. Laid out as a city in 1693, the year after the destruction of Port Royal by earthquake, it became the capital in 1872.

The city of Kingston is the capital of Jamaica because it is the centre of communications within the island and with the outside world. The main roads from the north, the east and the west converge naturally on the Liguanea Plain on which the city is built. The railway which is being revived after years of not operating has its terminus in the city.

Kingston's large sheltered harbour has made it possible for the city to be a major shipping centre for over three centuries. Its waters are sheltered by a long peninsula (a 'finger' of land projecting into the sea) called the Palisadoes. Esso Standard Oil Company built an oil refinery at the western end of the harbour. It was later purchased by the Government of Jamaica in 1982. The Norman Manley International Airport (formerly the Palisadoes International Airport) is located near the end of the Palisadoes peninsula and is one of the two international airports in the island. It is equipped to receive the most modern types of aircraft.

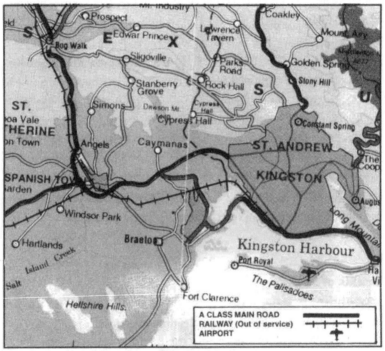

Kingston showing railway line, main trunk roads, airport

Kingston is a modern city built on a plain gently sloping upwards from the shores of the harbour northwards to the hills of St. Andrew. It is the seat of government and the centre of industry, commerce and culture for the whole island. The City of Kingston now extends to include the urban centres of St. Andrew, and is administered locally by the Kingston and St. Andrew Corporation (KSAC).

The city has numerous suburbs, and is steadily expanding north-wards as a residential area, eastwards as both residential and industrial

View of New Kingston

districts and westwards into Portmore and beyond. There has been special emphasis on large residential development in Portmore across the harbour from Kingston.

As Kingston steadily expanded, New Kingston, an extensive commercial centre, was built on what had been the Knutsford Park Race Course, midway between Cross Roads and Half-Way-Tree. Many commercial high-rise buildings have been erected for commercial firms, banks and insurance companies. Shopping centres, a supermarket and cinemas have been added. There are modern high-rise hotels in the Hilton Kingston, the Courtleigh and the Pegasus. New Kingston continues to expand to meet the growing needs of business and commerce.

Kingston's parochial buildings used to be looked after by two public bodies, the Kingston General Commissioners and the Mayor and Councillors. These have been replaced by single authority, the Kingston and St. Andrew Corporation. The Chairman of the Council is also the Mayor of Kingston. The St. Andrew Corporation came into being on May 1, 1933, when the parishes of Kingston and St. Andrew were amalgamated in order to secure better management of the affairs of both. Since then, Kingston and St. Andrew have been designated the Corporate Area. The combined population of Kingston and St. Andrew (1991) was 644,119 of which 562,073 lived in the metropolitan area called Greater Kingston, that is Kingston and urban St. Andrew.

Port Royal, formerly a separate parish but now part of Kingston, stands at the western end of the Palisadoes. The town has considerable historical and cultural significance. (See page 73).

ST. ANDREW

The parish of St. Andrew has an area of 455 sq. km (181 sq. miles) and a population of 540,715 (1991). It lies north of Kingston and stretches into the Blue Mountains.

Originally **Half-Way-Tree** was the parish capital and Cross Roads was also a town but now they have merged with and are regarded as extensions of Kingston itself. Lower St. Andrew is a populous residential area. The remainder of the parish, mostly rural, is given over to agriculture, its principal products being coffee, vegetables and ground provisions.

South of Papine and 11 km (seven miles) north-east of Kingston is the Mona Campus of University of the West Indies, occupying 259 hectares (640 acres) of the Liguanea Plain at the foot of Long Mountain. Nearby is the University of Technology.

In St. Andrew, bordering on Western Kingston, an industrial estate over 121 hectares (300 acres) in size was established by government to encourage the development of industrial plants outside of the business areas of Kingston and to facilitate the establishment of new industries using local and overseas capital.

Gypsum occurs in large quantities in eastern St. Andrew. The largest deposits are in the area of Bull Bay, within 3 km (1½ miles) of the coast.

The Right Excellent George William Gordon, one of Jamaica's seven National Heroes, was born in this parish in 1822.

ST. THOMAS

The parish of St. Thomas lies at the eastern end of the island, south of Portland, with the Blue Mountains forming its northern border. It has an area of 750 sq. km (300 sq. miles) and a population of 85,079 inhabitants (1991). The Chairman of the Parish Council is the Mayor.

Morant Bay, which lies on the coast road from Kingston, is its capital, chief town and shipping port. It has a population of 9,762 (1991). The bay is an open roadstead where large vessels can anchor safely. Seven miles east of Morant Bay is the town of **Port Morant,** which has a safe harbour with a deep-water pier on its eastern side at Bowden.

The town of **Bath** is famous for its sulphurous hot mineral springs and old Botanical Garden. Other principal towns and villages are Seaforth, Yallahs, Golden Grove, Cedar Valley, Easington and Trinityville.

An area of 175 sq km (70 sq. miles) from Silver Hill Gap in north St. Andrew to the coast of St. Thomas is administered by the Yallahs Valley Land Authority.

St. Thomas has two sugar factories and its main products are bananas, coffee, coconuts and sugar.

The Right Excellent Paul Bogle, one of Jamaica's seven National Heroes, is believed to have been born in this parish.

PORTLAND

The parish of Portland, which lies north of St. Thomas, extends from the highest peaks of the Blue Mountains down to the north coast. It is noted for its fertile soil, beautiful scenery and abundant rainfall.

Portland has an area of 820 sq. km (328 sq miles) and a population of 76,067 (1991).

Port Antonio is its chief town and capital, with a population of 13,205 (1991). It has two fine harbours, the western one being sheltered by a small islet called Navy Island. The town is divided into Upper and Lower Titchfield. Upper Titchfield occupies the peninsula and is the residential area; Lower Titchfield extends along the shore where the commercial section and municipal buildings are situated. Port Antonio is regarded as the cradle of the tourist industry in Jamaica. The Chairman of the Parish Council is the Mayor.

St. Margaret's Bay and **Buff Bay,** which lie on the old railway line between Kingston and Port Antonio, are thriving townships.

Manchioneal lies on the northeastern coast and is important mainly for bananas and coconuts.

The chief product of Portland is the banana. It was in this parish in 1868 that the banana trade with the United States was first started and developed into a major agricultural export crop. Coconuts are grown extensively.

Rafting is offered for recreation on the Rio Grande. Nanny of the Maroons, one of Jamaica's seven National Heroes, is believed to have been born in this parish.

Parishes of Middlesex

ST. CATHERINE

The parish of St. Catherine, which lies west of St. Andrew and south of St. Mary and St. Ann, is the largest parish in the island with an area of 1,260 sq km (483 sq. miles), and a population of 383,317 (1991).

Its capital is **Spanish Town,** originally built by the Spaniards who named in Santiago de la Vega. The name was changed by the British troops when they invaded the island and claimed it for England. The town was the capital of Jamaica until 1872 when the capital was moved to Kingston. It is built on the Rio Cobre Plain and is situated where the main route from the North Coast joins the southern plains. The population is 112,767 (1991).

Spanish Town, which has a Mayor, is of great historical significance. It contains what remains of the former Court House, House of Assembly and the original King's House (the Governor's residence) in the square dedicated to a British Admiral Rodney. There is also an impressive statue of Rodney who saved Jamaica from invasion by the French.

Spanish Town Square with Rodney Memorial

A four-lane highway connects Spanish Town and Kingston. Portmore, connected to Kingston by a causeway across Kingston

Harbour, has a population of 100,214 (1991) compared to 73,426 in 1982.

The northern road from Spanish Town passes through the picturesque gorge of **Bog Walk,** by-passes the township of **Linstead** and then continues to the bauxite town of **Ewarton** at the foot of Mount Diablo. On the southern road leading from Spanish Town is the town of **Old Harbour** which has 17,883 (1991) people. On the coast three miles from Old Harbour is Old Harbour Bay, the largest fishing village in Jamaica. It has a fine harbour with one of the best deep-water piers in the island. The main generating power plant of the Jamaica Public Service is in Old Harbour Bay.

Port Esquivel, where alumina is shipped from the island, **Lluidas Vale, Troja** and **Glengoffe** in the hills and **Port Henderson** and **Passage Fort** on the coast, are important areas. Many new industrial plants have been established in this parish.

The plains of St. Catherine, which provide numerous grazing areas, are largely given over to sugar and rice cultivation. The Rio Cobre Canal irrigates about 45,000 hectares (18,000 acres) of the St. Catherine Plans. The chief products of the parish are: sugar, rum, coffee, bananas, rice, citrus, tobacco and cocoa. Recently, fish farming has been introduced on an extensive scale. There are five sugar factories, an alumina plant at Ewarton, a citrus processing factory, a condensery and a pineapple-canning factory at Bog Walk (an important citrus area), a textile mill, a bagasse plant and a steel mill just outside Spanish Town. Bodles Agricultural Station is situated between Old Harbour and May Pen.

ST. MARY

The parish of St. Mary has an area of 634 sq km (254 sq. miles) and some 109,386 inhabitants (1991).

The capital of St. Mary is **Port Maria,** a town of 7,113 people (1991). The Chairman of the Parish Council is the Mayor.

Port Maria has a good harbour, partially sheltered from the "northers" by Cabaritta Isle which acts as a breakwater. **Annotto Bay** is on both the main road and the railway line between Kingston and

Port Antonio. The town is intersected by three slow rivers which create swamps in the surrounding area. There is a sugar factory at Gray's Inn to the west of Annotto Bay.

Oracabessa, which has a small but secure harbour, was once important as a banana ports. Tourism is now important there. The township of **Highgate** is situated eight miles from Port Maria on the road to Richmond, west of Port Maria. The area between **Boscobel** and **Tower Isle** has been developed into an important tourist resort.

The parish has a good variety of agricultural resources. The principal products are bananas, sugar, citrus, pimento, cocoa, coconuts and coffee. Copra is produced in fairly large quantities. The botanical gardens at Castleton are near the southern boundary of the parish.

The principal rivers from east to west are the Dry River, the Wag Water, the Rio Nuevo and the White River.

CLARENDON

The parish of Clarendon has an area of 1,167 sq. km (467 sq. miles). With a population which numbers 215,515 (1991) it is one of the most populous parishes in the island.

Its capital, **May Pen**, with a Mayor and a population 49,928 (1991) is situated on the banks of the Rio Minho about 56 km (35 miles) from Kingston, **Four Paths** is on the main road seven km (four miles) west of May Pen. **Frankfield** is the centre of a large and flourishing agricultural district. It has a railway station, which is the terminus of a 40 km (24-mile) long branch from May Pen to Frankfield and is the most important centre for buying bananas in the parish. Chapelton is the principal town of northern Clarendon, and was formerly the capital of the parish.

Spaldings is a thriving township with a healthy climate near the borders of Clarendon and Manchester. **Alley** is a small town on the banks of the Rio Minho; its economy depends almost entirely on the nearby sugar estates. The village of **Milk River** stands on the banks of the river whose name it bears. The Milk River Bath with its health-giving mineral springs is on the west bank of the river, five km (three miles) from the village.

Bauxite mining was established in the parish by JAMALCO and ALCOA. JAMALCO is an enterprise owned by the Jamaican Government and the Aluminium Company of America (Alcoa).

The Bull Head Mountains rising to a height of about 851 metres (2,800 feet) near the northern boundary of Clarendon, mark the geographic centre of the island.

Some of the island's tobacco is grown in Clarendon. The best sugar-cane cultivation may be seen in this parish, which produces the largest amount of sugar. May Pen is an important citrus packing centre. Copper-mining at Provost Keys and Retreat has been carried out from time to time over the years. The Denbigh agricultural showground is a short distance from May Pen. The Bustamante Highway connects May Pen to Mandeville.

ST. ANN

The parish of St. Ann, called "the Garden Parish of Jamaica" because of its extreme beauty, has an area of 1,200 sq km (481 sq. miles) and a population of 152,967 (1991). Bauxite and tourism play a major part in the economic life of the parish.

The capital town is **St. Ann's Bay** which has a Mayor and a population of 11,066 (1991). Less than a mile west of the town is the site of the first capital of the island, **Sevilla la Nueva** founded by Juan de Esquivel, the first Spanish Governor of Jamaica, in 1509. A shrine in honour of Christopher Columbus has been erected near there.

The world-famous Dunn's River Falls are located in the parish.

Dunn's River Falls, St. Ann

Ocho Rios about 10 km (7 miles) east of St. Ann's Bay, is an important tourist resort. Its harbour affords good shelter for ships, and it has fine deep-water piers for cruise ships and bauxite export. Its population in 1991 was 8,509. **Discovery Bay,** formerly called Dry Harbour is another town along the coast of St. Ann. Columbus is reputed to have landed there when he first anchored in Jamaica. Port Rhoades has been built here by Kaiser Company for the shipment of bauxite.

The road from Ocho Rios to **Moneague** in the interior passes through the celebrated **Fern Gully. Brown's Town** is the largest town in the interior of St. Ann with a population of 6,739 (1991). The township of **Claremont** once derived its importance chiefly from the nearby bauxite mines.

The agricultural products of the parish are chiefly bananas, pimento, sugar, coconuts and coffee. The soil is suitable for citrus and, in the drier areas, sisal is cultivated. Pimento grows abundantly in the parish which is also noted for cattle rearing.

The Right Excellent Marcus Mosiah Garvey, one of Jamaica's seven National Heroes, was born in this parish.

MANCHESTER

The parish of Manchester which lies between Clarendon and St. Elizabeth, has an area of 850 sq km (339 sq miles) and a population of 162,135 (1991). The parish offers considerable variety in climate, vegetation and scenery.

Mandeville, the capital and chief town of the parish, now has a Mayor. It is situated at an elevation of 626 metres (2,061 feet). The town is noted for its natural beauty and salubrious climate and is considered a fine health resort. It has a population of 41,741 (1991).

Christiana, 23 km (14 miles) north of Mandeville, is the second largest town of the parish. It is the centre of a large banana and ginger-growing district. The Christiana Land Authority assists agricultural development in the region. Irish potatoes are widely grown in the Christiana area. **Porus** near the eastern border of the parish, is a populous town on the railway line and the main road to the west.

Because the parish is extremely mountainous, there is no large-scale cultivation of crops such as sugar cane which require large tracts of flat land. Bananas, coffee and pimento are grown; the parish is noted for its oranges and ortaniques. There are no rivers in this parish and the southern districts often suffer drought.

The Right Excellent Norman Washington Manley, one of Jamaica's seven National Heroes, was born in this parish.

Parishes of Cornwall

ST. ELIZABETH

The parish of St. Elizabeth, situated between Manchester and Westmoreland has an area of 1,185 sq km (474 sq miles) a population of 144,384 (1991). Its capital and chief shipping port is **Black River,** a town of 3,427 people (1991), situated at the mouth of the river whose name it bears. The principal towns are **Lacovia, Santa Cruz, Newmarket, Siloah, Malvern** and **Maggotty.** On the northern boundary of the parish is **Accompong,** a Maroon settlement.

The northern and north-eastern section of the parish are mountainous. The central and southern sections form an extensive plain divided by the salubrious Santa Cruz Mountains. Although a large part of the lowlands is covered by morass, they provide some of the finest grazing land for cattle in the island. The Savannah of St. Elizabeth produces fine horses and mules.

Bauxite occurs in large deposits. **Port Kaiser,** near **Alligator Pond** has a leading deep-water pier for bauxite export. A huge plant for processing alumina has been constructed at **Nain.** There are two sugar factories in the parish and a tomato canning plant at **Bull Savannah.** Fishing is a major industry in the parish and rice cultivation has developed.

TRELAWNY

The parish of Trelawny has an area of 880 sq km (352 sq miles) and extends from the Cockpit Country to the north coast between St. Ann and St. James. Its population is 72,124 (1991).

The capital is **Falmouth,** a well laid-out town with a population of 8,066 (1991). It has a large harbour, the entrance of which has been enlarged. The town has a constant supply of water from the Martha Brae river.

Clark's Town, ten miles from Falmouth, and **Stewart Town,** near the eastern border of the parish, are important centres of trade in produce from the interior. **Rio Bueno** has one of the deepest harbours in the island. **Duncans,** near the coast, and **Albert Town** and **Ulster Spring** in the interior, are places which have grown in importance. **Troy, Wait-a-Bit** and **Warsop** are thriving villages in the Cockpit Country.

The only river of importance in the parish is the Martha Brae. The Dornoch water supply, one of the most successful water schemes established in the island, furnishes a large area of the lowlands with a good and wholesome supply of water.

Rum and sugar are Trelawny's principal products. There are two sugar factories in the parish. Other products are pimento, ginger and dyewoods. Some bananas are also grown.

ST. JAMES

The parish of St. James has an area of 600 sq km (240 sq miles) and 156,249 inhabitants (1991).

Its capital, **Montego Bay,** is known as "The Second City" after Kingston. It has a population of 85,503 (1991) and its residential areas are rapidly expanding.

The bay is an open roadstead opening to the west, protected by low hills from the trade winds, but partially exposed to the "Northers" between November and March. An elaborate deep-water pier has been constructed on reclaimed land which took in the area of the Bogue Islands. The city may be roughly divided into two sections: the tourist area occupying the northern section of the bay along the shore line, and the commercial and industrial sections which are second only to Kingston in size and volume of trade. The sea-bathing beach at **Doctor's Cave** is internationally famous.

Montego Bay is the most important centre of the tourist industry, and many modern hotels have been erected on the coast. North of the town is the Sangster International Airport.

Cambridge is next in importance to Montego Bay. **Ducketts, Seven Rivers** and **Chesterfield** which are areas of considerable rainfall, have large estates in banana cultivation. **Adelphi, Montpelier** and **Catadupa** are important townships.

The products of the parish are chiefly sugar, bananas and coffee.

The Right Excellent Samuel Sharpe, one of Jamaica's seven National Heroes was born in this parish.

HANOVER

The parish of Hanover at the western end of the island, north of Westmoreland, is the smallest parish in the island with the exception of Kingston.

The area of Hanover is 442 sq km (177 sq. miles) and it has 67,176 inhabitants (1991).

It is mountainous and well watered, although its rivers are small. The highest point in the parish is the Dolphin Head which serves as a landmark for ships. The beautiful beaches of Hanover offer considerable scope for the expansion of the tourist industry.

The capital town, **Lucea,** with a Mayor and population of 5,739 (1991) has a good harbour, narrow at the entrance but opening into a wide basin capable of receiving large vessels. It is almost completely landlocked. **Green Island** is a small shipping port. The village of **Hopewell,** about 24 km (15 miles) east of Lucea, is a major tourist resort.

Hanover is celebrated for its fine breeds of cattle. It produces chiefly bananas, ginger, sugar and rum, pimento, yams and arrowroot.

The Right Excellent Sir William Alexander Bustamante, one of Jamaica's seven National Heroes, was born in this parish. His birthplace at Blenheim has been converted into a National Shrine.

WESTMORELAND

The parish of Westmoreland, the most westerly in Jamaica, has an area of 800 sq km (320 sq. miles) and a population of 129,596 (1991).

Its capital and principal town is **Savanna-la-Mar,** with a population of 16,370 (1991). It is a shipping port and an important commercial centre. **Little London, Petersfield, Bethel Town, Williamsfield** and **Darliston** are the leading townships. Fishing is carried on at **Bluefield, Little Bay, Negril, Cave** and **White House.**

With its fertile soil and regular rainfall, Westmoreland is well suited for agriculture. It is watered by numerous rivers, chief of which are the Cabaritta, Roaring, Great, Negril and New Savannah. About 4450 hectares (11,000 acres) of the parish were once covered with morass lands which provided pasture for cattle in the dry season. In the recent past, the Government spent millions of dollars draining the vast areas in the vicinity of Negril. Roads, water and other facilities have been put in to provide for extensive tourist and other development. Nearly a quarter of the parish consist of alluvial plains suited for sugar cane while the remainder consists of hills of moderate elevation.

Sugar is the chief product of the parish, the main centre of which is at Frome where there is a large central sugar factory. Next in importance to sugar and its by-product, rum, is the cattle industry. Rice-growing has also been attempted, especially on the marsh land at the Paul Island district. Other products of the parish are bananas, ginger, pimento, logwood and honey.

Exercises on Chapter 4

1) What are the counties into which Jamaica is divided? Name the parishes of each county.

2) Why do you think Kingston is the capital of Jamaica? What advantages does its location offer? What is the population of Kingston? Where is Port Royal?

3) Where was the site of the first capital of Jamaica? What has been erected there?

4) What are the boundaries of St. Thomas? What is its chief town? Name its principal ports.

5) Give a general description of Portland. What is the chief product of the parish? Describe its capital. Name the main rivers of Portland.

6) What town was Jamaica's capital before Kingston? What do the plains of St. Catherine produce? Name and locate the chief towns of the parish.

7) What are the chief products of St. Mary? Name its chief town. Name its rivers.

8) What are the chief towns of Clarendon? What does the parish produce? Name two industries carried out in the parish.

9) For what is St. Ann noted? Name its chief towns. What are the chief products of the parish?

10) Give a general description of Manchester. Does it have any rivers? What are the geographical advantages of its capital? Which parts of the parish often suffer drought?

11) Describe the physical structure of St. Elizabeth. What are its major industries? Describe its capital.

12) What are the boundaries of Trelawny? Does the parish have a good water supply? What are its chief products?

13) Describe the capital of St. James. What are the chief features of the parish?

14) Give a general description of Hanover. What is its capital? What does the parish chiefly produce?

15) What is the chief industry of Westmoreland? Describe the physical structure of the parish. What is its capital?

16) What cities or towns have mayors? Which is the largest parish? Give its area. What is the smallest parish? Give its area. Which parish has the largest population? Which parishes are the largest banana producers? Which parish produces the most sugar?

17) Name Jamaica's seven National Heroes and the parishes in which they were born.

18) Draw the outline of the parish where you live, put on the capital of the parish and any other towns.

CHAPTER 5

INDUSTRY:
AGRICULTURE, TOURISM AND MINING

Agriculture

Agriculture is the basic industry of Jamaica. As the island possesses a wide variety of soil and climate, nearly every tropical product can be grown here.

The chief economic crops are sugar, bananas, citrus, cocoa and coconuts, each of which is dealt with below in detail.

Pimento is grown largely in St. Ann, Trelawny, Manchester and St. Elizabeth. Ginger grows well in Jamaica, especially at elevations of over 600 metres (2,000 feet) above sea level. Logwood, from which a dye is extracted, is found on the dry plains of St. Catherine, Clarendon and St. Elizabeth.

None of the major crops of the island is indigenous. Sugar cane, coconut, rice and ginger were introduced into the island from Far Eastern countries, bananas from the Canary Islands, cocoa from South America, limes and mangoes from India, the breadfruit from Tahiti and ackee from Africa.

SUGAR CANE

Sugar-cane, a tropical grass, can be grown under a variety of soil and climatic conditions. Alluvial plains containing large quantities of humus, as in St. Catherine and lower Clarendon, are very suitable. Flat or gently undulating lands are best; cultivation by hand or mechanical equipment and transportation of the reaped canes to the factory is more easily done on flat areas.

The manner of sugar-cane cultivation varies from district to district according to the conditions but the trend is towards more mechanization as dependence on hand labour grows less and less.

One important factor in sugar-cane cultivation is sunshine, which determines to a large extent the sucrose (sugar) content of the cane

juice. Flat lands always have more hours of sunshine than hilly districts. Before the introduction of heavy machinery, the small factories which crushed cane by windmills were usually situated on elevated land to make use of all the available wind. In recent times, however, the large central factories such as Frome and Monymusk are situated in areas to which transportation is relatively easy.

Sugar-cane is propagated by cuttings, and planted in rows about 4 feet 6 inches from each other. It requires intensive cultivation in order to produce satisfactory results. Moulding/mulching should be started when the plants are about 18 inches high, and the fields must be kept free from weeds. While irrigation is necessary on most estates, good drainage is essential and the soil must not be waterlogged. It is essential that the fertility of the soil be maintained by the addition of vegetable matter or artificial fertilizers.

The crop takes from twelve to eighteen months to reach maturity, and the first harvest reaped from the cuttings which have been planted are called plant canes. If the roots or "stools' are left in the ground, new shoots will grow from them. These are called ratoons. Fresh cuttings should he planted after the second ratoon, since the yield per acre diminishes rapidly after that.

By-products of the sugar industry are rum (for which Jamaica is world-famous), molasses, molascuit, a cattle food made of the interior cellulose fibre of the sugar-cane, power alcohol, and various forms of bagasse, such as the fiberboard known as "Celotex" and paper pulp.

CITRUS

The varieties of citrus may be divided into three classes: the orange, grapefruit and lemon. In the orange group, the types are the Common Jamaica, grown chiefly for home consumption; the Valencia, the fruit of which does not fall off the tree after ripening; the Navel, the Ortanique and the Seville. In the grapefruit group are the Marsh Seedless, the standard variety grown for export, the Silver Cluster and Duncan which contain many seeds, the ugli, chiefly exported, and the Chadwick.

The best soils for citrus are fertile, well drained, medium-textured loans with no impervious layer near the surface. Rocky hillsides with shallow soil exposed to erosion should be avoided. There should be about 125 cm (50 in) of rainfall evenly distributed throughout the years. The trees should be protected from prevailing winds and if there is no natural shelter by a mountain range or a belt of forest, windbreaks should be established before the orchard is started. Propagation is by budding.

BANANAS

Bananas are cultivated in nearly every moist tropical country, and constitute a substantial part of the local diet. Jamaica is one of the leading banana-exporting countries in the world.

Deep loam with a fair proportion of sand is the best type of soil for banana cultivation. There should be good under-drainage, for the roots are very susceptible to waterlogged soils. In Jamaica, bananas are grown on various kinds of soil, but especially on the three most important types — the alluvial soils, the shales and the red limestone soils.

The water requirement of the banana is very great. Whereas St. Mary and Portland with their abundant rainfall provide excellent banana lands, the St. Catherine plains have to be extensively watered by artificial means to grow bananas. A high temperature is necessary, and the plant thrives best in tropical and more so in equatorial climates. Clean weeding should not be practised.

The plants are propagated by shoots or "suckers" which used to be spaced 3 metres by 3 metres (9 feet by 9 feet) apart. However, closer planting with the use of fertilizers is now being done to get more yield to the acre. The plants are easily damaged by heavy wind and entire crops are destroyed in a hurricane.

Erosion is an important factor to consider in banana cultivation, for about 80 per cent of Jamaica's bananas is produced on sloping land. The plant does not provide protection against soil erosion, because its important roots occur in the top 10 to 24 inches layer of soil. Extensive conservation measures, therefore, have to be adopted on sloping ground.

Panama Disease and Leaf Spot are the two main diseases which affect the plant. The Lacatan variety of banana is immune to Panama Disease and while Leaf Spot is still a serious problem, it can be effectively checked by careful spraying. The main pest is the banana weevil borer, which can be controlled by strict field sanitation.

Packing bananas for export

COFFEE

Apart from its great demand on the world market, coffee is important as a "money crop" because it can be cultivated on slopes too steep for other crops, it can be picked by unskilled labour, it keeps well and is not damaged by rough transportation.

Coffee grows with best results in a warm, moist climate, and on rich, well-drained soils with an abundance of decayed vegetation. It is mainly a crop for high elevations and since it should be protected from wind, the leeward slopes of mountains are more suitable than the windward slopes. The large coffee-growing districts of St. Andrew are on the southern slopes of the Blue Mountains, thus sheltered from the North East Trade winds. Three chief chemicals should be present in the soil: potash, which is needed at all times, nitrogen and phosphoric acid.

One of the most important aspects of coffee cultivation is pruning, which gets rid of old wood and encourages new branches for blossoming and crop-bearing.

Blue Mountain coffee is of very fine quality, and in great demand throughout the world.

Cocoa

The original home of the cacao or cocoa tree is that part of South America watered by the Amazon and Orinoco rivers. In its wild state the cocoa tree grows under the shadow of taller trees. The tree which is about 15 to 30 feet high, begins to flower when it is about four years old, with blossoms arising from the trunk and branches which are more than a year old. Only 5 per cent of the blossoms usually set fruit, and the pods take about five months to ripen. Each pod contains twenty to forty-five seeds or "beans".

The varieties chiefly grown in Jamaica are the Forastero and Criollo. The cocoa tree will grow in a great variety of soils, provided they are deep and well-drained. The mean shade temperature should be about 80° F with an allowance of 15° F above and below this point.

Next to climate and soils, shade is the most important requirement for cocoa. In Jamaica, cocoa without shade suffers from dieback caused by the direct rays of the sun and by thrips, an insect attracted to unshaded cocoa. The most suitable shade trees are the quickstick or St. Vincent plum and the locust or cocoa oak. The guango or immortelle are also used. Temporary shade may be provided by plants such as the banana, pigeon peas and castor bean. Cocoa trees should be planted 4 metres by 4 metres (twelve feet by twelve feet) apart.

One important factor is that the cocoa tree suffers from the drying effect of continuous winds which injure the small, tender flowers and dry up the young pods. In the north of Jamaica where the northeast winds are prevalent, the cultivations must be protected either by hills or artificial windbreaks. The most important cocoa area in Jamaica is the parish of St. Catherine, which is sheltered from the trade winds by the central mountain range.

The principal cocoa harvest occurs between September and November, and there is a lesser harvest between February and April. Pods should be carefully cut to prevent damage to the tree. After having been processed extensively, the beans are finally used to make cocoa and chocolate.

There are four fermentaries in Jamaica for processing cocoa. They are situated at Richmond in St. Mary, Morgan's Valley in Clarendon, Haughton Court in Hanover and at the Cocoa Board's headquarters in the Industrial Estate in West Kingston.

COCONUTS

The coconut, the most widely cultivated of all the palms, grows best on alluvial soil which allows for free drainage. Coconut palms grow on many different types of soil but they give best results where the soil is friable (crumbly). Lands near the sea-coast are therefore the ideal soil for coconuts since the coconut is not susceptible to ordinary wind and requires heavy rainfall. The crop will thrive inland, however, where soil and rainfall conditions are suitable.

Formerly coconuts used to constitute a major part of Jamaica's export produce but now that the edible oil and soap industry has been developed, most of the annual crop is used in local factories.

In the 1970s, the tall coconut trees were afflicted by a disease called "Lethal Yellowing". Many thousands of trees were destroyed but replanting with resistant dwarf coconut trees and others which are immune to the disease has progressed rapidly.

FORESTS

The term "forest" here applies to lands with trees whose crowns cover more than 20 per cent of the land area. Jamaican forests consist of a mixture of mainly evergreen, broad-leaved tree species, with a sparse occurrence of more valuable species. This is a typical feature of tropical forests. In the 1970s as much as 24 per cent of the land area (267 hectares or 660,000 acres) was classified as forest and about 20 per cent (227 hectares or 560,000 acres) could be called wooded lands.

Jamaica is a very mountainous country, with more than two-thirds of the land mass above 300 metres (1,000 feet) in elevation. The forest cover is therefore extremely important in protecting the soil from severe damage by heavy rainfall and in conserving moisture which is allowed to percolate slowly into the natural aquifers and thus ensure continuous flow of the major rivers and streams.

In addition, these upland forests have a natural scenic beauty which is increasingly receiving the attention of the populace and tourists for recreational purposes. A number of recreational areas have been developed for public use within the national forest estate of 111,000 hectares (274,000 acres). Some are the Hollywell recreational ground just beyond Newcastle and the Blue and John Crow Mountain National Park.

The large area of forest land is managed by the Forestry Department, which was formed in 1942, and which has the responsibility of conserving and developing Government-owned forest lands. Since its formation, the Department has been encouraging private afforestation while carrying out its own afforestation programmes. There are now approximately 8,000 hectares (20,000 acres) of Government forest plantations, mainly Caribbean Pine (*Pinus caribaea*) and Blue Mahoe (*Hibiscus*). Studies carried out jointly by the Forestry Department and UN/FAO experts confirmed that the country has considerable potential to supply its future timber and wood requirements by large-scale planting of Caribbean Pine.

Jamaica's forests have always been exploited for timber but in recent years extensive clearing for agriculture, including coffee, and unrestricted cutting for other purposes have severely reduced the forest lands. Increased re-afforestation programmes are now being introduced, together with greater controls in the affected areas.

The Fishing Industry

Up to 1949, the Government had taken practically no active part in the Fishing Industry. In December of that year the Fisheries Division was set up as a sub-department of the Forestry Department. It was later transferred to the Department of Agriculture, which later became the Ministry of Agriculture and Lands.

Since December 1949, when the Fisheries Division of the Ministry of Agriculture and Fisheries was established as a branch of the Forestry Department, that Division has been actively engaged in the development and promotion of the Jamaican fishing industry by the provision of training and technical advice to fishermen, conducting exploratory fishing to test the potential of fishing grounds, provision of easy credit for outboard motors, duty-free outboard motor fuel, encouragement of fishermen's organizations such as co-operative societies, provision of outboard motor fuel outlets, gear stores, sanitary conveniences and lighting on beaches, and by the preparation and execution of schemes aimed at increasing the quantity of fish landed in Jamaica.

This Division is also responsible for the inland or fresh-water fisheries, and has been encouraging the cultivation of fish in ponds, tanks and marshes by provision of fingerlings and advice on pond management. Through this programme of fish-farming and the stocking of rivers and irrigation canals with fish, previously idle land has been put to more productive use, and a major source of cheap animal protein has been provided. This has had a significant effect on improving the diet of the people in several parishes of Jamaica, particularly St. Catherine, St. Elizabeth, Clarendon and Westmoreland. Since the 1980s, the inland fishing industry has developed to the extent that the import of fish for the tourist industry has been reduced. Up to the present, the inland fishing industry has shown an average of 4% annual growth.

In relation to the marine fisheries, the programmes carried out by the Government have produced results. Because of the training and advice given to fishermen, the fishing industry has extended its limits in that Jamaican fishermen are now able to fish at distances of up to 480 kilometres (300 miles) away from Jamaica, whereas thirty-five years ago they fished barely 16 kilometres (10 miles) away from shore. Today, fishermen are using synthetic materials for making their boats and equipment. Polythene rope has almost completely replaced Cayman rope among trap and pot fishermen, nylon and monofilament netting has taken over from cotton netting and, as it became more difficult to obtain the cotton and guango trees from which canoes were traditionally made, more and more canoes made of fiberglass have appeared on our beaches. As a result of Government assistance in obtaining credit, our fleet of large decked vessels grew in numbers and the fishing industry flourished. In recent years, however, the industry has been experiencing difficulties as a result of a reduced stock of fish and competition from foreign vessels fishing in Jamaican waters.

Tourism

Tourism is an important part of Jamaica's economy. Because of the island's warm climate and year-round sunshine, its beaches and beautiful landscape, many thousands of people from all over the world come here each year for a holiday.

Jamaica's tourism had its beginning in the latter part of the 19th century when invalids started coming to Jamaica to escape the cold winters in England and North America. The first tourist hotels were built in Montego Bay and Port Antonio. The now defunct Myrtle Bank Hotel in Kingston was built in 1892. In those early days, tourism was limited largely to the rich, the old, the few.

Tourism really began to prosper in Jamaica after World War I, when improved methods of transportation made it easier for people to travel from one country to the other. Indications are that in the early 1920s the number of tourists visiting the island annually probably did not exceed a few thousand. By 1938 the figure had risen to 64,000, and in 1952 the number of arrivals had almost doubled to over 104,000; in 1966 the number exceeded 345,000, and in 1970 it was nearly 415,000.

Cruise ship in Ocho Rios Bay

In 1982 it exceeded 600,000. Since the 1987–88 season the number of visitors has exceeded one million a year and has continued to grow, partly as a result of the great increase in the arrivals of cruise ship passengers. Total arrivals for 1993 were 1,616,340.

Mainly because of the white-sand beaches and pleasant weather, Jamaica's north coast has become the island's tourist centre, the main points being Montego Bay, Ocho Rios and Port Antonio. Many tourists visit Kingston too, but this city is most important as a commercial centre and the seat of government.

Today, tourism is Jamaica's largest earner of foreign exchange. Stores, restaurants, hotels, transportation, and many other activities that cater to tourists also provide direct employment in the industry.

Many other Jamaicans in every sector of the economy earn part of their income from tourism. For example, farmers supply food to the hotels and restaurants, and skilled carpenters make furniture; but there is no available estimate of this indirect employment.

The main marketing agency of the tourist industry is the Jamaica Tourist Board. Created in 1922 by Government as the Jamaica Tourist Trade Development Board, the present Board was re-organized in 1963 and a full-time Director of Tourism appointed. There is also a Ministry of Tourism.

Mining

Although there had been attempts for over a century to establish small-scale mining in Jamaica, the present well-established mineral industry dates back only to 1952 when the export of kiln-dried metallurgical bauxite ore was started. This was shortly followed by the export of alumina. The birth of this new industry was the result of successful exploration and development programmes. This development was somewhat unusual in that it occurred in areas near to well-established population centers with such infrastructure facilities as roads, railways and harbours. All these, of course, had to be vastly improved to service the new industry. Jamaica's mineral industry is mainly based on bauxite but it also includes industrial minerals such as gypsum, marble, silica sand and clays, and also a thriving sand and gravel industry.

Strip mining at Alcan

The occurrence and distribution of the ferruginous terra rossa soils which are rich in aluminium in Jamaica was noted by the West Indian Geological Survey. An English geologist, J.C. Sawkins stated in his *Geological Survey Memoirs* published in 1867 that the red earth was principally a mixture of iron and alumina. However, it was not until 1942 that attention was given to the economic significance of bauxite as an aluminium ore.

LEGISLATION

Under the Minerals (Vesting) Law, Chapter 251, the minerals are vested in and subject to the control of the Government. The principal mining legislation is the Mining Law Chapter 253, Law 41 of 1947. This was enacted after the Minerals (Vesting) Law and is supplemented by the Mining Regulations 1947 as amended by the Mining (Amendment) Regulations. The operations of quarries for many of the industrial minerals are controlled by the Quarries Law of 1955. Development of Petroleum resources is governed by the Petroleum Production Law Chapter 292.

BAUXITE AND ALUMINA

Characteristics of the ore: The bauxite deposits occur as solution cavity infillings within the members of the White Limestone Formation. The depths of the deposits vary from over 30 metres (100 feet) to only a few centimetres, but with an average depth of about 6 metres (20 feet). Deposits under 2 metres (five feet) deep are usually not considered mineable.

A study of the composition of the bauxite deposits in different areas of the island shows that there are distinct regional differences in the ore.

Companies: The commercial production of aluminium only began in the last decade of the nineteenth century though the existence of the metal in certain kinds of ore was known by scientists much earlier. However, until World War II (1939–45) greatly increased the demand for aluminium, little attention was paid to the rich deposits of bauxite outside Europe and the United States of America.

In 1942 a Jamaican businessman, Sir Alfred D'Costa, had soil tests done with a view to improving the fertility of his farm at Lydford in the parish of St. Ann. On analysis the soil proved to be highly aluminous and through the exertions of Sir Alfred and the colonial authorities (Jamaica then being a part of the British Empire) this fact was brought to the attention of aluminium producers in the Allied countries. The mineral was vested in the Crown in the expectation that it might be needed for the war effort.

Jamaican bauxite was in fact not used during the war but three North American companies – Alcan, Reynolds and Kaiser – came to Jamaica to survey, acquire reserve lands and set up operations over the next few years. Reynolds began exporting bauxite on June 5, 1952 from Ocho Rios and Kaiser followed a year later from a south coast port. Alcan built a processing plant near its mines at Kirkvine, Manchester and in early 1953 began shipping alumina, the intermediate product between the ore and the metal.

Production increased rapidly and by 1957 Jamaica had become the number one bauxite producer in the world with nearly five million tonnes, almost a quarter of all the bauxite mined in the world in that year. Alcan built a second refinery at Ewarton in St. Catherine in 1959, and in 1963 a fourth company, Alcoa, began mining in the island.

The production of alumina also increased, especially after the mid-1960s. By 1968 Alcan had brought the capacity of its refineries to over one million tonnes a year and, in 1969, a huge new plant was commissioned at Nain in St. Elizabeth by Alpart, a consortium of Kaiser, Reynolds and another US company, Anaconda. In 1971 Revere Copper and Brass opened the island's fourth alumina plant at Maggotty, St. Elizabeth. Two years later Alcoa, which had been shipping unprocessed bauxite since 1963, built the fifth refinery at Halse Hall, Clarendon, near the ancestral home of Sir Thomas de la Beche, one of the first of the great English geologists. As early as 1827, de la Beche had remarked on Jamaica's 'red, marly soils' in the first published notes on Jamaican geology.

By 1974 Jamaica had become the world's fourth largest producer and second biggest exporter of alumina. No smelters were built in Jamaica, however, and it is unlikely that any ever will be, largely because of two factors. The first is that aluminium smelting (or reduction) requires massive electrical energy; hence smelters are usually sited where there is hydropower, coal or natural gas. Jamaica gets its energy from imported petroleum. The second factor is that smelters are usually located in countries with a large market for aluminium.

The 1970s also brought other changes to Jamaica's position in the aluminium industry. In 1971 Australia overtook Jamaica as the leading producer of bauxite and that country now produces some 27 million tonnes a year as against Jamaica's 11 to 12 million tonnes. And in the past few years a West African country, Guinea, which has the world's highest grade bauxite, has also drawn ahead of Jamaica. The island's share of world bauxite output fell from 18.1% in 1974 to 9.0% in 1983.

Production of alumina rose by 45.1% to 2.2 million tonnes after a 6.3% fall in 1988. The year 1981 saw a 3.1% fall in bauxite but a 4.1% increase in alumina production. But between 1982 and 1984, during the world recession, both fell considerably. In 1989, bauxite began to recover with a 29.7% growth and alumina with a 45.1% growth.

The decline in the 80s was said to be due to varied and complex issues which included:

1) world economic conditions;

2) lower growth rates for aluminium;

3) energy availability and costs;

4) the decline of North America as a major aluminium and alumina producer — in particular, the Gulf Coast area;

5) take-or-pay contracts and consortia arrangements;

6) surplus of alumina on the world markets;

7) differential pricing policies.

Changes in Taxes and Ownership

During the 1970s there were important changes in the ownership of the Bauxite industry and its contribution to the Jamaican economy. Although the mineral had been owned by the state since colonial times, the companies exploiting it were wholly-owned subsidiaries of North American-based aluminium companies. Government purchased 51%

of Kaiser and Reynolds, 6% of Alcoa and 7% of Alcan, and repurchased most of the ore reserve lands formerly owned by the companies. In return, the companies were granted forty-year mining leases. In 1974, following dramatic oil price rises, the Government increased bauxite taxes by a Production Levy. The levy, in effect, indexes the price of bauxite to the price at which the companies sell aluminium ingot.

There are at present four bauxite and refining operations in Jamaica, Kaiser, Alcan, Clarendon Alumina Production Limited and Alpart. Reynolds ceased operations in April 1984 and Alcoa in February 1985. However, Alcoa has since resumed in partnership with Clarendon Alumina Production which is government owned.

The Government also set up new agencies to manage its enlarged interest in the industry. The principal of these, the Jamaica Bauxite Institute, began operating in 1976 to monitor, regulate, conduct research and advise the Government on all aspects of the industry.

Bauxite is mined by open-cast methods using the most modern large scale earth-moving equipment. The present emphasis is on blending to produce a uniform-grade ore, the use of lower grade bauxite, and the maximization of reserves. A benching method of mining, using power shovels and dragline is usually used. The ore is transported from the mine by a combination of rear dump off-highway trucks, belt conveyors, aerial tramways and railways. Ore for export is dried in rotary kilns to reduce the moisture content, while that for local processing is used as mined.

Restoration

Jamaica is almost unique in world mining history in that, at the inception of mining, emphasis was placed on the reclamation and rehabilitation of the mined-out bauxite lands. This programme has been singularly successful, in spite of the many problems involved. Further, the land between the pits is usually included in the reclamation programme. Grass is the crop usually planted on restored lands. Forest trees have also been established on restored lands, though in much smaller acreages than established in grass. Orchard crops have also been planted. About a half of the bauxite mined is shipped unprocessed to the United States. The other half is processed on the island in four alumina refineries which have a combined capacity of some 2.7 million tonnes a year. The alumina is exported mainly to Europe and North America.

Industrial Minerals

GYPSUM

This mineral occurs in the Port Royal Mountains of eastern St. Andrew where it is mined by quarrying. It is used in Jamaica as a retarder for cement. It is ground with cement in the proportion of approximately 1 part to 20 parts of cement. Most of the gypsum produced in Jamaica is exported to the USA, where it is made into plaster, which in turn, is used to manufacture wallboards. It is also used as a fertilizer.

SILICA SAND

Deposits of high grade quartz sand were discovered by the Geological Survey Department in May, 1958, in the Black River area. They occur as irregular patchy surface deposits in the gently undulating coastal plains. The purest sand is used for the manufacture of flint glass for the container industry. It is important that this sand contain iron oxide in order to produce a colourless glass. The less pure sand is used as foundry sand, while the finer fraction may be used as an abrasive in soap powder.

CLAYS

Deposits of clay occur in several areas of the island. The best is in the Hodges area where it is associated with the silica sand. The clay shrinks considerably on drying, and this presents problems in its utilization. At present small pockets of clay are used by art potters and small operators to make traditional Jamaican clay ware.

Minerals for Construction

CEMENT

The manufacture of Portland Cement was started under licence granted in 1949. Limestone, the major raw material, is quarried at Long Mountain and conveyed about 1.7 miles to the plant where it is crushed and mixed with clay dredged from the harbour, or with shale from nearby areas. Expansion of the plant has taken place and now includes a belt conveyor system for movement of raw materials and the construction of a clinker plant able to process 900,000 tonnes per annum. The growth of the industry has paralleled the growth of the construction sector.

MARBLE

Marble, which is suitable as ornamental stone, is found in Serge Island, Mount Auburn and adjacent areas of St. Thomas. The colour varies from almost white — occurring at Bath, St. Thomas — to black near Clydesdale and Tweedside. The coloration is due to accessory minerals in the marble.

LIMESTONE AND LIME

Limestone is our most abundant mineral. The White Limestone provides the rocks most frequently used. These vary from chalky to marly beds and some contain flint nodules. Even the best of the hard limestone is usually well fractured. Apart from being essential to the production of cement, limestone is also used in building construction and as a fill in road construction. In a few localities, the limestone has a beautiful pink colour but in general it is white.

Some horizons of the limestone are extremely pure and are used in the manufacture of lime. This is a major raw material in the alumina industry. Lime is also used in agriculture, sugar-refining, glass-manufacture and building.

SAND AND GRAVEL

Deposits of natural sand and gravel occur in St. Catherine, St. Andrew, Westmoreland and St. Elizabeth areas. Elsewhere, crushed and sized limestone is used for the same purposes as sand and gravel.

METALS

Copper minerals occur in Upper Clarendon, particularly in the Charing Cross—Bellas Gate area, in the Rio Grande and Swift River districts in Portland, and in the Port Royal Mountains of St. Andrew. Most of these occurrences have been known since about 1869, but as yet no economic deposits have been located although the Charing Cross and Standford Hill Mines in Clarendon were operated briefly during the latter part of the last century and between 1906 and 1909.

There are known occurrences of lead and zinc with some copper and arsenic at Rock Castle in the Hope District of St. Andrew. This deposit was first worked during the eighteenth century and abandoned. Mining was again resumed about 1856 but the mine was closed by about 1860. There are at present remains of the adits, crushing mill, and a concentration plant.

Small high-grade deposits of iron ores occur on both slopes of the Blue Mountain Range, and concentration of magnetite-ilmenite sands occur particularly as beach placers. The largest is in the Alligator Pond area. Most of these areas are currently under licence and are being prospected.

PETROLEUM

There has been exploration for petroleum both on-shore and off-shore. The Windsor Spring near St. Ann's Bay and carbonaceous shales are perhaps the best indication that petroleum could occur in Jamaica, but as yet too few wells have been drilled for any firm decision to be made on the probability of finding petroleum here.

Recent Developments

A notable development in Jamaica's export economy since Independence has been the development of non-traditional exports. These include flowers and ornamental plants, specialized tropical fruits, art and crafts. Growth industries include garment manufacturing, particularly as a result of the Caribbean Basin Initiative, data processing, music and entertainment.

Exercises on Chapter 5

1) Write an essay on the importance of agriculture in the economy of Jamaica.

2) Show why the island can produce a wide variety of crops. Are its economic crops indigenous?

3) What are the conditions under which sugar-cane grows best? In what parishes would you expect to find the sugar estates of the island? Name the by-products of sugar.

4) What are the best conditions for banana cultivation? Explain why Portland and St. Mary produce the most bananas.

5) How would you choose a site for a cocoa cultivation?

6) What factors must be considered in picking a location for citrus? How is citrus propagated?

7) What are the best conditions for coffee cultivation?

8) Describe the nature of the soils on which coconuts grow best. Why has coconut export diminished.

9) What practical purposes do forests serve?

10) Tell what you know about fishing in Jamaica.

11) Describe briefly the minerals which are mined in Jamaica.

12) Why is the mineral industry important to Jamaica?

13) What minerals are present in bauxite?

14) What happens to the land after bauxite is mined?

15) Name two of Jamaica's non-traditional exports.

16) When and how did Jamaica's tourism industry begin?

17) Where were the first tourist hotels built?

18) How does tourism aid other sectors of Jamaica's economy?

CHAPTER 6

GOVERNMENT, PUBLIC UTILITIES AND COMMUNICATIONS

How Jamaica is Governed

Jamaica as an independent country since August 6, 1962, is governed entirely by Jamaicans, without interference from anyone outside, on the basis of the Rule of Law set out in the Constitution which became effective at midnight on August 5, 1962.

The system of government is called "democratic" because the government is elected by the people themselves every five years, everybody in Jamaica aged 18 or over having the right to vote. This is called universal adult suffrage. The Parliament (that is, the Government of Jamaica) consists of Her Majesty, a Senate and a House of Representatives. The Queen is represented in Jamaica by the Governor General, who is appointed by her on the recommendation of the Prime Minister.

The Senate (also called the Upper House) consists of 21 persons, called Senators, all appointed by the Governor General on the advice of the Prime Minister and on the advice of the Leader of the Opposition. The Senators among themselves choose a chairman who is called the President.

The House of Representatives (also called the Lower House) consists of 60 members (called Members of Parliament or MPs) who are elected by the voters of Jamaica every five years. They select their own chairman who is called the Speaker.

The responsibility of Parliament is to look after the welfare of the island and its people. It makes the laws and handles the finances of the country. In the maintenance of law and order, Parliament is assisted by the Judiciary (that is, the Courts), the Police Force and by the Jamaica Defence Force and other military units with regard to the defence of the island.

The principal instrument of policy-making is the Cabinet which is charged with the general direction and control of the Government of Jamaica and whose members are collectively responsible therefore to Parliament. The Cabinet is headed by a Prime Minister, appointed by the Governor General from the members of the House of Representatives. The Prime Minister is the person whom the majority of the Members of Parliament choose as their leader. In addition, there are no fewer than 11 other members, all appointed by the Governor General on the advice of the Prime Minister, from among members of the two Houses, (Senate and House of Representative) no fewer than two and no more than three such ministers being members of the Senate. The members of the Cabinet are the Ministers of Government. In the running of the country's business the Civil Service is the principal factor of assistance to Parliament.

Ministries are formed and may change from time to time but, regardless of how many Ministries there may be, the following always exist:

> Ministry of Finance (whose minister *must* be from the House
> of Representatives)
>
> Ministry of Health
>
> Ministry of Education
>
> Ministry of Agriculture
>
> Ministry of Foreign Affairs
>
> Ministry of Labour
>
> Ministry of Trade

All Prime Ministers become members of the British Privy Council and carry the title "The Right Honourable" for life.

PARISH COUNCILS

Besides the Parliament (sometimes called the Central Government) with headquarters in Kingston, the capital city, there are also the Parish Councils which are elected every three years. Each of the fourteen parishes elects a Council to handle matters of local government. Kingston and Urban St. Andrew are grouped together for this purpose and called the Corporate Area which is administered by the Kingston and St. Andrew Corporation, the chairman of which is the Mayor who is chosen each year by the members of the Corporation Council.

The Chairman of a Parish Council is generally elected as the Mayor of the capital town of the Parish (where such towns enjoy mayoral status).

The Parish Councils receive money from the Central Government which the latter collects as parish rates and trade licences and also it gives grants to the Parish Councils, as available, to carry out their work. The chief work of the Parish Councils is to look after local interests within the boundaries of the parishes in connection with such matters as the care of the poor, sanitation, garbage collection, street cleaning, maintenance of parochial roads, public health and such amenities as parks and markets and abbattoirs and other local matters.

An important part of their work is to supervise the construction of new buildings, the development of land and other matters of public welfare.

PARISH CUSTODES

In each parish, citizens recommend persons perceived to be of sober character and high integrity to the police for appointment as Justices of the Peace (J.Ps) or Lay Magistrates. The police then recommend the appointment of such persons to the Governor-General, after due investigation into their background. The Governor-General, at his discretion, appoints a senior Justice of the Peace within a parish as its Custos.

Justices of the Peace or Lay Magistrates preside over petty sessions courts, witness signatures of persons signing documents and assist the police in various areas of their duties.

Dependencies of Jamaica

With the coming of Independence to Jamaica, the Turks and Caicos Islands, 750 km (450 miles) to the north-east of Jamaica, and the Cayman Islands, 295 km (178 miles) to the north-west of Negril Point, ceased to be Dependencies of Jamaica. They reverted to the charge of

Britain, although by agreement the Government of Jamaica continues to assist them in judicial and police matters, when invited to do so.

THE MORANT AND PEDRO CAYS

The Morant Cays are small uninhabited islands, four in number, situated about 55 km (33 ml) to the south-east of Morant Point. In May and June, innumerable sea-birds called boobies used to flock these islands. Their droppings (known as guano when dry) make a valuable manure which was once used on some of the sugar estates of Jamaica. The eggs of these birds used to be collected sold in Jamaica as "booby eggs". However this caused a decrease in the number of birds being born, so the practise is now outlawed.

The Pedro Banks are an important fishing area. The Pedro Cays, four in number, also uninhabited, lie 65 to 80 km (40 to 50 ml) to the south of Pedro Bluff in St. Elizabeth. These cays lie on the Pedro Banks, a vast shoal extending from a point 65 km (40 ml) south of Portland Point, westward for 250 km (150 ml).

Public Utilities

ELECTRICAL POWER

Historical and Current Development

The first public electricity supply was produced in 1892 from the Gold Street Power Station by The Jamaica Public Service Light Company. In 1898 the West Indian Electric Company started an electric tramway system to serve the Kingston area. In 1923 the Jamaica Public Service Company (JPSCo.) was incorporated and acquired the assets of the West Indian Electric Company. At that time, only a few isolated areas outside of Kingston and St. Andrew and Spanish Town had electricity service provided by relatively small organizations. Between 1930 and 1956 all of these small companies producing electricity were acquired by the Jamaica Public Service Co. Ltd.

In the late 1950s, legislation was introduced and a commission created to carry out a change in the supply frequency from 40 Hz to 60 Hz to a standard islandwide frequency of 50 Hz. This conversion was completed by the end of 1962.

In 1966 JPSCo was granted an exclusive twenty-five year franchise which made it the sole supplier of public electricity in Jamaica. The Jamaica Government also created at that time an independent public utility commission to regulate the operations of the company.

During 1974, the Electricity Authority (a Government Agency) made an offer to purchase outside ordinary stock of the JPSCo. At the present time the government is the owner of approximately 99% of the issued ordinary capital of the company, through the Electricity Authority and the Accountant General.

JPSCo operates under a 39-year "All-Island Electric Licence" granted by the Government on August 31, 1978. Until 1989, JPSCo was subject to regulation by the Ministry of Public Utilities. In 1989, the Ministry of Public Utilities was merged with the Ministry of Mining and Energy. This move ensures that portfolio responsibility for all major elements of the energy sector is vested in the Ministry of Public Utilities, Mining and Energy.

Plant Expansion

Since receiving the "All Island Electric Licence" in 1966, the company, with the cooperation of the Government of Jamaica, has secured major loans for development. In 1966 the first Power Project Loan was obtained from the International Bank for Reconstruction and Development (IBRD, and also referred to as the World Bank). Two electric generating units with a total capacity of 93 Megawatt were constructed at the Old Harbour Power Station with the associated transmission and distribution facilities. The first Power Project financed by the World Bank (Loan No. 454-JM) was completed in 1970.

In March 1970 financing was finalized for the construction of a 68 Megawatt Steam Electric Generating Plant, Unit No. 3, at the Old Harbour Power Station with the necessary transmission and distribution facilities.

In March 1973 the company embarked on the development of a new Power Station in Kingston. In 1976, a 68.5 Megawatt Stream Electric plant was installed at Old Harbour and the Hunt's Bay B6 unit was installed and commissioned.

Also in 1976 a Rural Electricity Programme (REP) was started. This programme, initially financed by a loan from the Inter-American Development Bank (IDB), had two objectives. Firstly, the programme was aimed at raising the standard of living of rural dwellers and secondly to halt or substantially reduce the migration of human resources from the rural areas to the metropolitan areas, Kingston in particular.

In 1978 a second Power Project Loan was entered into (Loan No. 1516-JM) for the development of the company's transmission, substation, distribution and general property facilities.

In 1982 a third Power Project Loan (No. 2188-JM) entered into with the World Bank was used to finance rehabilitation of power plants and construction of transmission, substation and distribution facilities.

In September 1985 the Company, through a loan from the Japanese Government, commissioned a floating Power Station consisting of two 20 megawatt slow-speed diesel generators at the Rockfort Power Station in Kingston. The construction expenditure between 1986 and 1993 was as follows:

1986	$ 73.2 Million
1987	$119.5 Million
1988	$132.6 Million
1989	$117.3 Million
1990	$220.2 Million
1991	$563.9 Million
1992	$971.5 Million

While the numerous rivers of the island may be looked upon as sources of hydro-electric power, most of them cannot be exploited because their flow is not constant throughout the year. The station on the Rio Cobre, which was laid down in 1898 and was one of the oldest Hydro Electric Plants in the Western Hemisphere, was closed in August 1966. There are eight Hydro Electric Stations which are located as follows: Upper White River – Ocho Rios; Roaring River – St. Ann; Lower White River – St Ann; Maggoty – St Elizabeth; Rio

Bueno – Trelawny; Constant Spring – St Andrew; Rio Bueno 'B' – Trelawny; Ram's Horn – St Andrew.

Hurricane Gilbert in September 1988 damaged considerable sections of the company's transmission and distribution facilities. This necessitated significant restoration expenditure.

In October 1990 the company's generating capabilities and reliability were improved with the addition of two gas turbines (Units 6 & 7) at Bogue Power Station in St James, providing 18.5 Megawatts each.

In 1992 two gas turbines (Units 8 & 9) were installed at 18.5 Megawatts and 324.5 Megawatts respectively.

In December 1993 gas turbine No.10 was installed at Hunt's Bay in Kingston providing 32.5 Megawatts.

WATER SUPPLIES

The water supply for Kingston and St. Andrew is drawn principally from the Hermitage Dam 21 km (12.75 miles) from Kingston and 580 m (1740 feet) above sea level. This dam takes the waters of the Wag Water, Ginger and Moresham rivers.

The dam is about 233 m (700 feet) long and 47 m (142 feet) from the bottom to the crest. It can store 350 million gallons of water. Desilting has been done. The Mona reservoir (formerly named the Richards Reservoir for Sir Arthur Richards, a former Governor of Jamaica) is situated in lower St. Andrew and stores 825 million gallons of water, part of which began to be harnessed from the Yallahs River in St. Thomas in 1984.

In October 1980 the National Water Authority, which was responsible for water supplies to rural areas, and the Water Commission, which was responsible for supplies to the Corporate area, were merged and are now the National Water Commission.

In 1986, the responsibilities of operating and maintaining the rural water supply were transferred from the Parish Councils to the NWC.

In 1989, some of the minor supplies were re-assigned to the Parish Councils, while the NWC operates and maintains the major supplies for the country.

In order to ensure that the quality of water distributed to the public is safe and aesthetically acceptable, the Commission has established and maintains and operates two water quality laboratories, one in Kingston and St. Andrew and one in Montego Bay. Water samples are taken daily and submitted to these laboratories for bacteriological and chemical analyses.

A Ministry of Water was established in 1998.

Communications

In Jamaica there are two main ways of travel: by road and by air (the railway which is non-functional at present, is being revived). Geographic structure determines to a large extent the communications within a country. In this island, travel by water, except along the coasts, is negligible; the rivers are precipitous and their courses are often broken by waterfalls.

ROADS

The central mountain system running East to West divides the island into north side and south side. Consequently, the system of main roads was originally a belt around the island near the coast. Of this main system, there are three principal crossings from South to North, one through Stony Hill from Kingston to Annotto Bay, the second over Mount Diablo, from Spanish Town to St. Ann's Bay, the third from Savanna-la-Mar to Montego Bay by way of Mackfield.

With this main structure as a basis, other main roads with a total length of approximately 4,515 km (2,720 miles) link up every major town and village. Roads designated as main roads are traffic arteries outside the Corporate Area of Kingston and St. Andrew, maintained by the Public Works Division of the Ministry of Works. In addition, there is a road network of approximately 10,800 km (6,500 miles) maintained by the Parish Councils, called parochial roads, and which include some 3,300 km (2,000 miles) of bridle and foot-paths.

RAIL

The route of the now dormant railway, once operated by the Jamaica Railway Corporation, was largely decided by the structure of the country. Owing to the island's mountainous nature, there are numerous tunnels on the lines. The chief centres of population on the north coast are Montego Bay and Port Antonio, which are connected by the main railway routes to Kingston on the south coast.

A short sub-spur branches from the Port Antonio line at Bog Walk for a distance of 10.4 km (6.25 miles) to Linstead. The total length of the railway lines is 340 km (205 miles).

Since 1992, the railway has not been in operation except for the sections on which bauxite is drawn to Port Esquivel, from where Alcan ships bauxite.

AIR

Air Jamaica Express provides scheduled domestic service from the Tinson Pen aerodrome to the Sangster International Airport (Montego Bay) and connects Boscobel (Ocho Rios) and Ken Jones (Port Antonio) aerodromes.

There is also a Jamaica Flying Club with its base at the Norman Manley International Airport.

Several international airlines provide international services to Jamaica. International airlines serving Jamaica are: American Airlines, Air Canada, Air Jamaica, British Airways, BWIA, Cayman Air Lines, Mexicana and Cubana.

BUS SERVICES

Corporate Area

In Kingston and St. Andrew, a bus service was provided by Jamaica Omnibus Services Limited, under a fifty-year exclusive licence granted by the Government made effective December, 1953. The service covered the urban and suburban parts of the Corporate Area and gradually extended to rural parts of St. Andrew. The Company operated a fleet of over 400 buses on some 38 routes in the Corporate

Area. But this system was changed in 1984. Independently owned buses and minibuses now serve these routes under licence from the government, and are monitored by the Transport Authority.

Rural

Almost all main routes into and through the rural areas are served by motor omnibuses, either owned by Limited Liability Companies or individuals, and operated under licences.

POSTAL COMMUNICATION

This important department includes the Money Order and Parcel Post Service, as well as the ordinary mail service. There are 310 post offices; 463 postal agencies and 34 sub-agencies in the island. Mail is received daily in all the important towns and villages and distributed by mail coaches throughout the island. There is a house-to-house postal delivery in the major towns.

TELEPHONE

Cable and Wireless (Ja) Ltd. with headquarters in Kingston, maintains a local and international telephone, and telegraph system which connects every important town in the island. All of the principal post offices have call boxes. Telephone calls can also be made via satellite to any country in the world. Cable and Wireless also provides Internet connections for the island.

RADIO AND TV

There are seven broadcasting stations in Jamaica: Radio Jamaica owned by the public, workers of RJR and a number of organizations; privately-owned stations – KLAS in Mandeville, Irie FM in Ocho Rios, Hot FM in Montego Bay, Power 106, and Love FM, a religious station.

There are two television stations: TVJ, formerly JBC TV, which was government-owned but now owned by RJR, and CVM TV.

PRESS

There are three daily newspapers, the *Gleaner* and the afternoon *Star,* published by the Gleaner Company and the *Jamaica Observer* which began life as a weekly paper in 1992. The *Western Mirror* in Montego Bay is published twice weekly. There are a few weekly newspapers, including the *Sunday Herald,* which was formerly a daily newspaper and the *Children's Own,* published by the *Gleaner* during school term.

Exercises on Chapter 6

1) Give a short summary of how Jamaica is governed. What is the Cabinet? What are Parish Councils?

2) Name the Ministries of Government. Who are the Ministers now?

3) Name the company which is responsible for generating and supplying electricity throughout Jamaica.

4) How is the Corporate Area supplied with water?

5) When was the National Water Commission established?

6) What services does Cable and Wireless Jamaica provide?

7) What are the principal means of communication in the island?

8) What service does the Postal Department provide?

9) How does the telephone help in island communication?

10) What is known as 'The Press'?

SECTION 2: HISTORY OF JAMAICA

INTRODUCTION

The recorded history of Jamaica may be roughly divided into six periods. The first period may be said to date from Columbus's arrival in the island in 1494 to the destruction of Port Royal in 1692. Very little is known about the days when the Spaniards were masters of Jamaica. On the other hand, a good deal is known about the first fifty years of Jamaica as a British colony.

The second period of our history extends from the destruction of Port Royal to the abolition of the slave trade in 1807. During this time Jamaica flourished as an agricultural colony and became very rich. For most of those years 'Sugar was King' although coffee, cotton, indigo, annotto, logwood, spices and other tropical products were also exported. The island reached the height of its prosperity just before the slave trade was abolished; that is, just before the British government decided that no more slaves were to be brought from Africa and sold as private property.

The third period of Jamaican history covers the years between the abolition of the slave trade and the Morant Bay Rebellion in 1865. During the fifty-eight years between the abolition of the slave trade and the Rebellion, the country passed through many misfortunes and there was a great deal of misery and ill-feeling among the different classes of people in the island.

The fourth period dates from 1865 to the end of July, 1914, during which time Jamaica was ruled by Britain as a Crown Colony. The fifth period began with the outbreak of World War I on August 1, 1914 and ended in August 1962.

The sixth period began on August 6, 1962, when Jamaica became an independent country. All the events which took place after that date are part of Jamaica's post-Independence history.

CHAPTER 7

COLUMBUS TO THE DESTRUCTION
OF PORT ROYAL

The Spanish Period

In 1494, on May 5, Christopher Columbus arrived at the island of Jamaica. This was on his second voyage to the New World, which was afterwards called America. Columbus annexed the island in the name of his master and mistress, King Ferdinand and Queen Isabella of Spain. But it was not occupied until Juan de Esquivel came from Santo Domingo in 1509. For 146 years, Jamaica remained a Spanish colony.

A Young Christopher Columbus

When Columbus first set foot on a Jamaican beach, the island was then inhabited by a gentle race of people called the Arawaks or Tainos. They had come from the country now known as Guyana, where Taino Indians are still to be found. They were short, copper-coloured people, rather stout, with straight black hair and flattish noses. They lived in huts shaped like those the peasants of Jamaica who came after them used to build and they slept in hammocks. They made rough seats of wood, and spears tipped with stone, or with the teeth of sharks. They did not have the bow and arrow. The men were skilful fishermen, and caught fish and turtles to eat. They made their cooking vessels out of clay, and hardened them with fire. The women grew cassava, corn and sweet potatoes for food. Cotton grew wild in the island, and they twisted the fibre into cloth, strips of which they wore around their waists. They also wore strings of beads and shells.

They were peaceful people and not accustomed to working hard. But the Spaniards made slaves of them and put them to difficult tasks. The Spaniards treated the Arawaks so harshly that in about fifty years all of them were dead. They had numbered fully sixty thousand. The Spaniards got slaves from Africa to take their place.

The Spaniards first settled on that part of the northern coast of Jamaica which is now known as the parish of St. Ann. There they built a town called Sevilla Nueva, or New Seville.

Afterwards they moved to the southern part of the island and built the town of St. Jago de la Vega (St. James of the Plain), which is still called Spanish Town. The island was given to the Columbus family as a personal estate in 1540, but they did nothing to develop it. The Spanish colony in Jamaica was never a very large or a very flourishing one.

The English Arrival

In 1655 on May 10, a body of English sailors and soldiers landed at what is now called Passage Fort, in Kingston Harbour, and marched towards Spanish Town. They were commanded by Admiral Penn and General Venables, who had been sent by Oliver Cromwell to capture the island of Hispaniola from the Spanish. Penn and Venables failed to take the city of Santo Domingo and sailed on to Jamaica. On May 11, the Spaniards surrendered. They were allowed a few days to leave the island. Some of them went to Cuba but others secretly went to the north side of Jamaica, along with their African slaves who became the first Maroons of Jamaica.

In the month of October, General Sedgwicke arrived from England and took charge of the colony. Many of the English sailors and soldiers, and the people who came with Sedgwicke, died from the fevers of the country and the hard food and water they consumed. Sedgwicke himself died shortly after his arrival, and General Brayne was sent out to manage the affairs of the colony. He expected he would be attacked by the Spaniards of Cuba, and so he fortified the positions occupied by the English. General Brayne died in 1656, and General Doyley, an officer of the army, became Governor.

SPANISH RESISTANCE

In 1657 Don Cristobal Arnaldo de Ysassi led strong guerrilla forces in the interior. He had been appointed the last Spanish Governor of Jamaica. Two expeditions from Cuba came to the north coast to help him. General Doyley attacked both times by sailing around the island from Kingston. He defeated Ysassi near Ocho Rios in 1657 and at Rio Nuevo in 1658, the last named being the biggest battle ever fought in Jamaica. Ysassi continued to hold out until 1660, when the defection of the Maroon allies made his cause hopeless, and he and his followers escaped to Cuba in canoes.

In 1661 a Commission arrived from England formally appointing Doyley as Governor of Jamaica, and commanding him to establish a Council to assist him in the government of the colony. This Council was to be elected by the colonists.

In 1662 Lord Windsor arrived as Governor of Jamaica. He brought with him a Royal Proclamation declaring that all children born of English subjects in Jamaica should be regarded as free citizens of England. Lord Windsor retired from the Government of Jamaica within the year, and Sir Charles Lyttleton became Deputy Governor. There were then 4,205 persons in Jamaica. Santiago de Cuba was captured and looted by Admiral Myngs.

In 1663 an expedition sailed from Jamaica to attack the Spanish town of Campeche, in Central America. After some misfortunes, this effort succeeded, and much booty and many ships were taken by the English. In the same year we first hear of the English trying to suppress the Maroons. These Maroons were descendants of former slaves of the Spanish. They had escaped to the mountains and forests in the interior, where they lived a wild, free life and, it was rumoured, murdered every white person they came across. An expedition was sent against them under Juan de Bolas, a former Maroon who had aided the English. The soldiers were defeated. Peace was patched up shortly afterwards between the Maroons and the English, but it did not last for long.

The first House of Assembly was called together. It consisted of twenty members elected by the colonists. It met at Spanish Town and passed forty-five laws for the government of the colony.

Sir Thomas Modyford arrived from Barbados with a thousand settlers. He was a Barbadian planter and had once governed Barbados. He was sent to Jamaica as Governor. He helped and protected the English buccaneers under Henry Morgan who had moved to Port Royal from Tortuga. The ships and plunder they brought vastly enriched Port Royal. Modyford encouraged agriculture, especially the cultivation of cocoa and the sugarcane. During this time a large number of slaves were brought from Africa to Jamaica. But the slave trade with Jamaica had already become established.

In 1668 Henry Morgan, the famous buccaneer, who had his base at Port Royal attacked and plundered Porto Bello on the Isthmus of Panama.

In 1671, leading a body of buccaneers from Jamaica, Henry Morgan attacked and captured the old city of Panama. After plundering it, he burned the city to the ground and returned to Port Royal with an enormous amount of loot.

In 1673 there were 17,272 persons in Jamaica. In that year Sir Henry Morgan became Lieutenant Governor.

In 1674 Lord Vaughan arrived as Governor. The next year 1,200 settlers from Surinam came to Jamaica and started sugar planting.

In 1677 Sir Henry Morgan once more became Lieutenant Governor after Lord Vaughan left Jamaica. He was again Lieutenant Governor in 1680.

In 1678 the Earl of Carlisle arrived as Governor. He brought with him instructions that before any laws were passed by the House of Assembly, a draft of them should be submitted to the King for his alterations or approval. Before this, the House of Assembly had first passed laws, and then sent them to England for the King's approval. The House strongly protested against this change, which would have reduced its power and authority very much. After a long struggle, the English Government yielded, and the old system was continued.

In 1687 the Duke of Albemarle arrived as Governor. With him came Sir Hans Sloane as his physician. Sir Hans Sloane wrote two large volumes on Jamaica. Albemarle favoured Sir Henry Morgan, who died in 1688 and was buried with honours at Port Royal.

In 1690 the Earl of Inchiquin arrived as Governor. During this year a rebellion of the slaves took place at Chapelton in Clarendon. It was suppressed, and the ringleaders were executed. Some of the slaves, however, escaped to the mountains, where they joined the Maroons.

In 1692 Sir William Beeston Became Governor of Jamaica.

THE PORT ROYAL EARTHQUAKE

On June 7, 1692 the great Port Royal earthquake occurred. Port Royal was then the chief city in Jamaica, famous for its riches. The House of Assembly met there. The buccaneers took their prizes there. The houses were substantially built of stone. The inhabitants lived a wild, reckless life, and Port Royal was described as one of the wickedest places on earth.

At about 20 minutes to 12, on the forenoon of June 7, the inhabitants of the town were startled by a noise like thunder, which seemed to come from the north. Immediately the earth began to shake, and then the walls of the houses fell on every side. There were three shocks. The first was not very severe; the last was the worst. As it was built on sandy soil, a considerable portion of the city sank beneath the sea. The sea receded, then rushed back with terrible force, sweeping over the land and drowning hundreds of persons. Thousands perished. Minor shocks occurred all that day and for several days afterwards. The earthquake was felt all over the island; great landslides occurred and some springs disappeared. The dead bodies of the people floated in the harbour and rotted on the land. Port Royal was almost completely ruined. Its surviving inhabitants endeavoured to restore what was left of it to its former importance, but in 1704, a fire broke out in one of its warehouses and destroyed every building except the forts.

Many people fled Port Royal after the earthquake and settled across the harbour on the site which is now Kingston.

Exercises on Introduction and Chapter 7

1) Into how many periods may the history of Jamaica be divided? How many years did the first period cover? How many years did the second? The third? When did the fourth begin and end? The fifth? What particular significance is attached to the sixth period?

2) When did Christopher Columbus arrive in Jamaica? What were the first inhabitants of Jamaica called? State briefly what you know about them. How were they treated by the Spaniards?

3) In what part of the island did the Spaniards first settle? What was the name of the town they built there? To what part of the island did they afterwards go? What was the name of their new town?

4) In what year did the English capture Jamaica? Name the commanders of the English expedition. Why had they come from England?

5) Say what you know about General Sedgwicke. Who was Don Cristobal Arnaldo de Ysassi? Who defeated him and where?

6) In what year was General Doyley formally appointed Governor of Jamaica? In what year was issued the Proclamation declaring all freeborn English subjects in Jamaica citizens of England? What was the population of Jamaica in that year?

7) When was Campeche attacked? What caused Port Royal to become famous? When and where did the first House of Assembly meet? Who was Sir Thomas Modyford? State briefly what he did as Governor of Jamaica.

8) What was the population of Jamaica in 1673? Say what you know about Sir Henry Morgan. When did the Earl of Carlisle become Governor of Jamaica? Describe the instructions to the House of

Assembly that he brought with him. How did the House of Assembly receive those instructions?

9) Describe the rebellion that took place in 1690. Who was Governor then? State what you know about the Maroons.

10) When did the great Port Royal earthquake occur? What sort of place was Port Royal then? Say what you know about the effects of the earthquake.

JAMAICAN HISTORY PART 2: 1693–1782

CHAPTER 8

FOUNDATION OF KINGSTON TO THE
BATTLE OF THE SAINTS

Introduction

When the earthquake destroyed Port Royal, Jamaica was already becoming known as a great sugar-producing country. Many sugar estates were being cultivated, and sugar was being sent away to be sold in England. Cocoa was also grown, and sarsaparilla. Horses, cattle and pigs were plentiful.

There were three classes of people in the island. The first class were the white men, who owned property, or who had professions and trades. They were well-off and spent their money freely. They were not careful in their habits, and so they died at an early age as a rule.

The second class also consisted of white men; but these were almost slaves. It was the custom in those days to send to the American colonies people who in Great Britain had been convicted of some crime. These were "deported" for five, seven or ten years, and were bought for those years by planters who wanted men to work. They were treated as slaves; but, if they lived long enough, they regained their freedom after they had served their time. Free men in England could also sell themselves for a number of years to planters in Jamaica, and during those years they were little better than slaves.

The third and largest class of persons in Jamaica were the slaves brought over from Africa. They had to work very hard; they were given poor food; and very few of them could ever hope to be free. But, as time went on, they were treated less harshly.

In 1696, four years after the destruction Port Royal, there were 47,365 people in Jamaica.

Rallying to the cause of the slaves were the Maroons who were descendants of ex-slaves who had fled to the hills following the British take-over of the island in 1655. At the beginning of the eighteenth century, one of the outstanding Maroon leaders was Nanny, a Chieftainess of Nanny Town in the Blue Mountains. 'Granny Nanny', as she was fondly called was known by both the Maroons and the British settlers as an outstanding military leader who became, in her lifetime and after, a symbol of unity and strength for her people during times of crisis.

In 1693 the year after the destruction of Port Royal the city of Kingston was laid out. The ground on which the city now stands was then covered with trees and grass-pieces, and was a large private property. It was marked off into streets and lanes, and buildings began to be erected. Kingston soon became an important town.

In 1694 England and France being at war, a French fleet under Admiral Du Casse attacked Jamaica. During a whole month, this fleet landed men on the north and east coasts of Jamaica and plundered the plantations there. On July 19, 1,500 Frenchmen landed at Carlisle Bay in Clarendon. Here they were opposed by two hundred colonists and some slaves. Later on, several hundred more colonists arrived on the scene and, after a few days' fighting, the French were driven back to their ships. They had destroyed fifty sugar estates and fifty plantations. They captured and took away over 1,300 slaves.

In 1702 Admiral Benbow sailed from Port Royal in search of the French fleet under Du Casse. He caught sight of it near the coast of Colombia, and attacked it at once. For five days the fight continued, the English ships pressing the Frenchmen hard. On the fifth day Benbow's leg was broken by a shot. He wanted to go on fighting, but two of his captains, named Kirby and Wood, persuaded the English ships to withdraw. The English ships returned to Port Royal where the two captains were tried for their conduct and shot. Benbow died a few months after. He was buried in the Kingston Parish Church, where his bones still lie.

In 1704 Colonel Handasyd became Governor. He retired in 1711. All during his government there was trouble in Jamaica. The Maroons were very active and made attacks on the estates and their owners. The members of the House of Assembly quarrelled with the Governor. Agriculture did not prosper, and there was general distress.

In 1711 Lord Archibald Hamilton became Governor. In that same year a great storm swept over the parish of Westmoreland and destroyed a vast amount of property and took many lives. The next two Governors, Peter Heywood and Sir Nicholas Lawes, were planters and appointed from Jamaica. Heywood served from 1716 to 1718.

In 1718 Sir Nicholas Lawes became Governor. He introduced coffee into Jamaica three years later. During his time pirates worried the planters on the coast lands very much. Sir Nicholas Lawes did a good deal to suppress diem.

In 1722 the Duke of Portland arrived as Governor. During his a dministration the parishes of Portland and Hanover were formed. The first, Portland, was named for him. In this same year, but before the Duke's arrival, a terrible hurricane swept over Jamaica, and caused great destruction of life and property.

In 1728 Major General Hunter arrived as Governor. During his time the Maroons were very troublesome. Two regiments of soldiers had to be brought from Gibraltar to protect the Jamaican planters and their estates against them. The Maroons were commanded by a man named Cudjoe, and as they knew the country perfectly, they always managed to escape when pursued. Bloodhounds were imported to hunt them down; but it was not until 1734 that any victory was won over them. In that year a body of soldiers attacked a Maroon village called Nanny Town and destroyed it. A good many Maroons were killed. Many Maroons threw themselves down the precipice which their town overlooked rather than become prisoners.

Granny Nanny of the Maroons

But the Maroons were not crushed. They rallied again, and when another expedition of 200 sailors and 400 militia men was sent against their new town, they surrounded these forces and attacked them. The Maroons were hidden among the rocks and trees, and thus could not be seen. Twenty men were killed and many wounded on the English side before the troops managed to escape.

In 1738 Edward Trelawny became Governor. He governed the island for nearly fourteen years, and was one of the ablest Jamaican administrators. On his arrival, he tried to bring the Maroon War to an end. A determined effort was still being made to subdue these people. Mosquito Indians from Nicaragua were employed to hunt them down, along with the Jamaican militia. But a colonist, Guthrie by name, conceived the plan of making the Maroons the friends of the Government. His idea was acted on by Governor Trelawny and a treaty of peace and friendship was drawn up between the Maroons and the Government. The Maroons were given land in different parts of the country, free of taxes. They were allowed to govern themselves. They were to be tried and punished by their own chiefs, but no chief could pass the sentence of death on any of them. By the terms of the treaty, they were to capture all runaway slaves and take them back to their owners. They were also to assist in suppressing any rebellion among the slaves.

In 1741, war having broken out again between England and Spain, Jamaican troops took part in Admiral Vernon's disastrous attempt to capture Cartagena. Governor Trelawny personally led a regiment to the Isthmus of Panama the next year, but soon returned, unsuccessful.

In 1744 on October 20, Jamaica suffered from storm and earthquake. Port Royal and Kingston were severely affected and Savanna-la-mar was destroyed. Twelve persons were drowned.

In 1746 an insurrection of the slaves broke out. This led to the passing of laws inflicting terrible punishment on those rebelling against their owners.

In 1751 Governor Trelawny left the island. His relations with the House of Assembly had been cordial and he was liked and respected by the people.

In 1752 Admiral Knowles became Governor. During his administration (in 1754) Kingston was temporarily made the capital of the island. Four sessions of the House of Assembly met there.

In 1760 a formidable insurrection of the slaves took place in St. Mary under a leader called Tacky. They seized the town of Port Maria, armed themselves, murdered all the white people that fell into their hands, and were preparing for further outrages when they were met by the troops sent against them. They fought desperately, but in the end they were defeated. Four hundred were killed in battle and six hundred were deported to British Honduras. The ringleaders were put to death.

In 1762 William Henry Lyttleton became Governor. In that same year an expedition against Cuba left Jamaica. Troops had been raised locally, composed of coloured freemen and slaves who were promised emancipation. Havana was captured, but was afterwards restored to Spain when peace was made between that country and England.

In 1764 the population of Jamaica was estimated at 166,454. Of these, 140,454 were slaves. In the following year, the House of Assembly wanted to limit the number of slaves to be imported in the future, but the Governor would not agree.

In 1766 Mr. R. H. Elletson was appointed Lieutenant-Governor. In that same year a hurricane swept over the west end of the island.

In 1767 Sir William Trelawny became Governor. At first he quarrelled with the House of Assembly, but afterwards and until his death, there was peace between the House and the Governor.

In 1772, when Sir William Trelawny died, the House of Assembly voted a thousand guineas for his funeral. It was in his honour that the parish of Trelawny was formed and named. Lieutenant Colonel John Dalling acted as Governor after Trelawny's death.

In 1774 Sir Basil Keith arrived as Governor.

The House of Assembly again passed Bills to restrict the importation of slaves into Jamaica. But the British Government would not allow these Bills to become Law. There were now 209,617 persons in the island. Of these, 192,787 were slaves. Sir Basil Keith died in 1777.

In 1778 war was declared between England and France during the revolution of the thirteen colonies in North America against England. A French fleet sailed for the West Indies, and most of the small British West Indian islands were captured. Jamaica was thrown into a state of excitement and alarm. Martial Law was proclaimed. Colonel Dalling was again acting as Governor, and he vigorously prepared for the defense of the colony. Fortifications were strengthened and the Militia was improved by drill and discipline. Horatio Nelson who later became a famous British Admiral was then on West Indian service. He was made Governor of Fort Charles in Port Royal, in 1779. The French fleet, however, did not attack Jamaica.

In 1780 an expedition against the Spanish colony of Nicaragua left Jamaica. Horatio Nelson went with it. San Juan was taken. Nelson returned to Jamaica, and for some time lay seriously ill at Port Royal.

A terrible hurricane devastated the parish of Westmoreland: £40,000 was sent from England for the relief of the sufferers. The misery caused by this calamity was very great. The town of Savanna-la-Mar was again completely destroyed.

In 1781 General Archibald Campbell became Lieutenant Governor.

A humane law was passed by the House of Assembly. Up to this it had been legal and customary to mutilate slaves convicted of grave offences by cutting off ears or hands. The new law now rendered such mutilation illegal. There was another severe hurricane.

In 1782 Rodney won his celebrated victory over the French Admiral, the Compte de Grasse in the Battle of the Saints. De Grasse had intended to invade and capture Jamaica, and the colonists were in a state of fear and trepidation until the news of Rodney's victory was received. The great battle was fought off Dominica on April 12. The French Admiral's plan was to avoid meeting Rodney until he could join his allies, the Spaniards, whose fleet lay off Haiti. Rodney was determined, if possible, to prevent this meeting. He followed the French as fast as he could, and, in spite of the wind being against him at first, caught up with them at the islets called the Saintes near Dominica. A bloody naval engagement followed. The French were completely beaten. Some 3,000 out of the 6,000 men intended for the invasion of Jamaica were killed or wounded. Rodney brought the captured ships to Port Royal, and the grateful colonists voted £3,000 for the erection of a marble statue in his honour. The statue now stands in the Square in Spanish Town. The British Government made Rodney a peer. His victory saved Jamaica from a French invasion.

Exercises on Chapter 8

1) What town grew up to replace Port Royal? What was the size of the population of Jamaica in 1696?

2) In what year did Admiral du Casse attack Jamaica? When did the Frenchmen land at Carlisle Bay? What happened then? How many plantations and estates did they destroy? How many slaves did they capture?

3) When did Admiral Benbow sail from Port Royal in search of the French fleet? Where did he meet it? Describe what happened then. Where did Benbow die, and when?

4) When did Sir Nicholas Lawes become Governor? What crop did he introduce into the island?

5) When did General Hunter become Governor? Describe the troubles with the Maroons during his administration.

8) When did Edward Trelawny become Governor? What arrangement did he make with the Maroons? Who was Guthrie?

9) When did Governor Sir Edward Trelawny leave the island? What important event took place while he was Governor?

10) What did the slaves of St. Mary do in 1760? What was their leader called? How many were killed? What happened to their ringleaders?

12) What was the population in 1764? How many of the people were slaves?

13) When did Sir William Trelawny become Governor? What were his relations with the House of Assembly? What did the House of Assembly do when he died?

14) Describe the events of 1778.

15) What humane law did the House of Assembly pass in 1781? How had rebellious slave been punished before the passing of this law?

16) In what year did Admiral Rodney defeat the Compte de Grasse? Where was the battle fought? What did Jamaica do to show her gratitude to Rodney? Was his victory important?

CHAPTER 9

RODNEY'S VICTORY TO ABOLITION OF THE SLAVE TRADE

Introduction

After Rodney's victory over De Grasse, the French and Spanish Governments made no further serious attempt to capture Jamaica. France was soon to have very grave troubles of her own, for in 1789 the great French Revolution began, and two years later there was a rebellion in Haiti, which was the first step taken towards the independence of that country. And Spain, conquered by Napoleon after the French Revolution, afterwards lost her extensive possessions in South and Central America.

Great Britain had also suffered a severe loss in 1776. In that year the American Colonies declared themselves independent of the Mother Country. Canada remained subject to Great Britain and many of the American loyalists moved to Canada rather than become subjects of the American Republican Government. Some of these Loyalists also came to Jamaica, and some went to the Cayman Islands with their slaves.

The agitation against the slave trade, and against slavery itself, had already commenced. In 1772 Lord Mansfield and other learned English judges declared that the moment a slave set foot in England he became a free man. This judgment was the result of the effort of Mr. Granville Sharpe to secure the liberation of three Jamaican slaves taken to England. In 1777 a Mr. Hartley moved a motion in the British House of Commons that "The slave trade was contrary to the laws of God and to the rights of man." The motion found no support. Then, in 1789. Mr. William Wilberforce moved twelve resolutions in the House of Commons, all against the slave trade, and from that time forward the fight against slavery continued until its final abolition in 1838.

In 1783 General Campbell was appointed Governor of Jamaica.

On February 5, Prince William Henry, afterwards William IV, visited Jamaica. He was the first Royal Prince to come to the this island.

In 1784 General Alured Clarke became Lieutenant Governor.

On July 10 and 30, severe storms occurred. In the following year another storm swept over Jamaica. This was followed by a drought in 1786, then in October of the same year there was another storm. The result of these repeated calamities was awful. It was calculated that, since 1780, fully 15,000 slaves had perished from want, caused by the destruction of the provision fields and the plantations. Owing to the separation of America from England, there was no trade between Jamaica and America, and so food could not be imported from the latter country.

In 1790 the Earl of Effingham arrived as Governor. He was received with festivities. It was then the custom to welcome Governors with three days of feasting in Spanish Town and two in Kingston. Nearly £4,000 was voted by the House of Assembly for this purpose, but after the arrival of the Earl of Effingham the Assembly decided that this expenditure must cease.

The Earl of Effingham died within a few months of his arrival in Jamaica.

In 1791 General Williamson became Governor.

The white planters in Haiti, who were opposed to the French Revolution and who objected to their slaves being set free eventually appealed to England for help. France, now a republican country, became involved in war with England and other European states. Some of the French Royalists came over to Jamaica to ask for aid. They offered Haiti to the British Crown.

In 1793 a detachment of British troops and black soldiers went from Jamaica to Haiti. Some important Haitian cities were captured, but the troops died rapidly from disease.

Lord Balcarres succeeded General Williamson as Governor of Jamaica. General Williamson again led a military expedition into Haiti but did not succeed in capturing the island. The English were eventually defeated and expelled by Toussaint l'Ouverture.

Trouble arose between the Government and the Maroons of Trelawny. The Maroons complained that they were not being properly treated. Two Maroons had been flogged in a local workhouse instead of being handed over to the Maroons to be dealt with, as they ought to have been. They also asked for more land, as their numbers had increased. The Governor did nothing to make peace. He preferred to fight the Maroons, and so a new Maroon War broke out.

About 5,000 troops were employed against the Maroons, and bloodhounds were imported from Cuba to hunt them down. A reward of £10 was offered for every Maroon captured.

For some months the struggle continued without any clear victory. At last the Maroons of Trelawny surrendered, having been promised that they would be allowed to remain in the island. This promise was broken. They were shipped away to Canada, and from there they were sent off to Sierra Leone on the west coast of Africa. As the Maroons in the other parts of the island had not been concerned in this war, they were left undisturbed. They continued to enjoy the rights and privileges they had won during the administration of Governor Sir Edward Trelawny.

In 1798 there was a slave uprising in the parish of Trelawny. It was soon suppressed. The colonists were also very much alarmed by rumours to the effect that the victorious republicans in Haiti were endeavouring to stir up a rebellion among the slaves in Jamaica. Two men from Haiti were arrested on a charge of conspiracy, and one was hanged.

The people of Jamaica raised a very large amount of money to assist England in her war with France. The sum is said to have been £80,000.

In 1801 General Nugent arrived as Lieutenant Governor.

In 1803 Kingston was made "a corporate city," that is, a city with a Mayor, twelve aldermen, and twelve councillors. These formed the governing body of the city.

The largest crop of sugar ever produced in Jamaica was exported.

In 1804 two hurricanes occurred.

In 1805 Martial Law was proclaimed in Jamaica. England and France were at war, and a French fleet had been sent into West Indian waters. This fleet was not intended to capture the islands but to destroy as much property as it could, and to draw the English fleet from European waters, since Napoleon was planning to invade England. After ravaging Dominica, the French fleet returned to Europe. This fleet was defeated by Lord Nelson at the Battle of Trafalgar.

In 1806 General Nugent left Jamaica, and Sir Eyre Coote succeeded him as Lieutenant Governor.

SLAVE TRADE ENDED

In 1807 the Slave Trade between Africa and Jamaica was abolished by the British Parliament. It was decreed that, after March 1, 1808, no more slaves should be brought to the island. Thus the first part of the fight against slavery was won by the abolitions.

It has been estimated that from the time that Jamaica passed into the hands of the English until the abolition of the slave trade, over one million human beings had been imported from Africa. When the trade was abolished, there were 319,351 slaves in the island.

Exercises on Chapter 9

1) Why was no serious attempt made to capture Jamaica after Admiral Rodney's victory?

2) What territorial loss did Great Britain suffer in 1776?

3) What do you know about the agitation in England against the Slave Trade?

4) In what year did Prince William visit Jamaica? What happened in Jamaica owing to the storms and hurricanes which occurred from 1780 to 1786? Why could no food be imported from America?

5) When did the Earl of Effingham arrive as Governor? How was he received? How were Governors welcomed in those days?

6) When did Lord Balcarres become Governor of Jamaica? Why did trouble arise just then between the Maroons of Trelawny and the Government? What was the Governor's attitude? How many troops were employed against the Maroons? How much money was offered for every Maroon captured? What happened to the Maroons who surrendered? What happened to those who did not rebel?

8) What were the outstanding events of 1805?

9) When was the Slave Trade abolished? How many slaves were there in Jamaica when the slave trade was abolished?

CHAPTER 10

DECLINING IMPORTANCE, EMANCIPATION, MORANT BAY REBELLION

Introduction

The destruction of Napoleon's French fleet at Trafalgar by the British in 1805, and the subsequent defeat of the French off Santo Domingo by Admiral Duckworth (February 6, 1806), resulted in Jamaica ceasing to have to provide largely for her own defence. During the years when Napoleon's ships were moving over the waters of the Caribbean, this Colony sometimes spent as much as £20,000 a year for the support of the soldiers maintained here. This huge expenditure gradually ceased after the defeat of Napoleon at sea, and his later downfall.

Jamaica's importance as a military and naval station declined during the nineteenth century. The wealth which came to this island through its being made, at the time of the Napoleonic wars, a depot for goods to be smuggled or sold to the neighbouring Spanish-American countries, diminished also. Twenty years after the Battle of Trafalgar the Jamaican planters began to complain bitterly of poverty. The great days of Jamaica's prosperity were over. Her days of adversity had begun.

The abolition of the slave trade also brought about considerable changes in the treatment of the slaves. It no longer paid the planters to work a slave beyond the limits of his endurance. As no more workers could be imported from Africa, the value of those in the island increased greatly. The slaves were allowed a small piece of land on the plantations on which they worked, and they could cultivate this bit of land one day in every two weeks. They were allowed to sell what remained of the provisions they grew, after taking enough for their own support. Thus a good many slaves acquired money. These either bought themselves out of slavery, or purchased the freedom of their children, before abolition took place.

In 1808 The Duke of Manchester, who also held the title of Viscount Mandeville, arrived as Governor. In the same year there was a mutiny among the men of the 2nd West India Regiment, which was stationed at Fort Augusta. The mutiny was chiefly confined to the recruits, who were Africans. The older soldiers remained faithful, and shot down the mutineers.

In 1809 a conspiracy of the slaves in Kingston to burn down the city and murder the white inhabitants was discovered. The ringleaders were put to death.

In 1814 the Baptist Mission was founded, and the largest coffee crop ever reaped in Jamaica was shipped away.

In 1815 Simon Bolivar, the Liberator of Spanish Central America, came to Jamaica as a political refugee and remained for about seven months. The Duke of Manchester entertained him. This was the year of the Battle of Waterloo.

Simon Bolivar

In 1816 the law was rescinded which stated that the owner should pay £100 to the Government for giving a slave his liberty. This law had been passed to prevent owners from liberating too many of their slaves.

In 1818 Jamaica was struck by two severe hurricanes, one in October and another in November.

In 1819 the Government made a determined effort to exterminate the gangs of runaway slaves who roamed the country and robbed travellers, stole cattle and whatever else they could put their hands upon. These slaves numbered nearly 2,600. Many of them were captured or slain.

In 1820 the Duke of Manchester fell from his horse and fractured his skull. He left the island for a time, and General Conran became Lieutenant Governor.

In 1823 the House of Assembly refused to accept the British Government's instructions to make easier the condition of the slaves. The House of Assembly declared that the code under which the slaves were governed was calculated "to render the slave population as happy and comfortable, in every respect, as the labouring class in any part of the world." The planters objected to the British interfering in any way with themselves or their slaves.

In 1824 the Presbyterian Church of Jamaica was founded.

The year after, Jamaica was constituted an independent Episcopal See, and the Rt. Reverend Christopher Lipscombe, D.D., came to Jamaica as the first Bishop of the Anglican Church.

In 1827 the Duke of Manchester retired from the Governorship of Jamaica after having governed the island for nineteen years. The parish of Manchester and the town of Mandeville had both been named for him. Major General Sir John Keen became Lieutenant Governor.

In 1829 the Earl of Belmore arrived as Governor. The year after his arrival there was a hurricane.

In 1830 a great insurrection of slaves broke out in St. James and rapidly spread to the parishes of Trelawny, Hanover, Westmoreland St. Elizabeth and Manchester. For many years the agitation against the treatment of the slaves in Jamaica had been going on in England with increased vigour. The oppression of the slaves by Jamaican planters was violently denounced in England by the abolitionists, and in Jamaica the planters talked loudly of the injustice to which they were subjected in England. The slaves heard of what was taking place in England, and some of them believed that the King had granted them freedom and that they were being wrongly kept in bondage by their owners.

In 1831, December 28 marked the beginning of the last great slave rebellion. It was reputed to have been instrumental in bringing about the abolition of slavery. Led by Samuel ('Daddy') Sharpe, a Baptist Deacon, this Christmas Rebellion lasted for four months until the rebel leaders were overpowered and hanged in Charles Square, Montego Bay, later renamed Sam Sharpe Square. Samuel Sharpe was hanged on May 23, 1832 and was buried in the sands of the Montego Bay Harbour from which his remains were later recovered and interred beneath the pulpit of the Burchell Baptist Church. The missionaries working among the slaves were accused of having been the indirect cause of this insurrection, and some of them were very harshly treated.

Sam Sharpe

In 1832 the Earl of Belmore left Jamaica, and the Earl of Mulgrave arrived as Governor. He urged upon the House of Assembly the necessity of adopting measures looking to the better treatment of the slaves. The House returned a petulant answer. It denied the right of the British House of Commons to assume any power of supremacy over the colonists of Jamaica, and it declined to act on either the suggestions of the Governor or the resolutions of the House of Commons. The British Parliament then determined to act decisively.

Edward Jordan, a light-coloured freeman who had served all liberal causes, was tried for his life for the stand taken by his newspaper, *The Watchman*. He was acquitted but given a prison term on other trumped-up charges.

Apprenticeship

In 1833, in the month of May, the English Colonial Secretary stated in the House of Commons that all appeals to the slave-holders had been made in vain, and that the British nation must now, on its own initiative, suppress slavery in all the British Dominions. The Abolition Act was passed on August 28. It enacted that all children under six years of age should be set free. There was to be a six years' period of "apprenticeship" from 1834 to 1840, after which every slave in the British Empire should receive full freedom. The British Parliament voted £20,000,000 as compensation to the slave-holders in the Empire. Of this amount, £5,853,975 was the share that fell to the Jamaican slave-holders.

In 1834 the Marquis of Sligo arrived as Governor. The apprenticeship system began under him.

On the 1st of August, 1834, all the chapels and churches in the island, except one or two churches in Kingston, were opened for Divine Service. These places of worship were attended by thousands of the people. On the following Monday the "apprentices" turned out to work, except in the Parish of St. Ann. In two or three other parishes some minor disturbances occurred later. On the whole, it was soon found that the apprenticeship system was not working well. The planters, angry that they had been defeated in their struggle to maintain slavery, inflicted numerous punishments on the apprentices. Consequently it was determined, by the British Parliament in 1838, that the period of apprenticeship should cease on the 1st August, 1838.

On September 13, the first issue of *The Daily Gleaner* was published.

THE GLEANER,

And Weekly

COMPENDIUM OF NEWS.

PRINTED AND PUBLISHED
BY JACOB DeCORDOVA.   *Pick'd from the chaff and ruin of the times,*   *EVERY SATURDAY AFTERNOON*
To be new varnish'd.—SHAKESPEARE   *WATER LANE.*

Vol. 1 Saturday Afternoon, September 13th, 1834. No. 1.

First Issue of *The Gleaner*

Emancipation

In 1838 on August 1, Emancipation Day, there were demonstrations throughout the island to celebrate the first day of complete freedom. In Spanish Town, the capital, a hearse containing the chains and shackles that were sometimes put on rebellious slaves was driven through the streets, and these symbols of slavery were solemnly buried. There were bonfires and feasting everywhere. Queen Victoria who had lately ascended the throne, was blessed as the author of the people's freedom.

But the troubles which had begun during the time of the apprenticeship, now became much worse. Many of the free people did not wish to work for the men who had once owned them. There were complaints about the small wages that the planters offered: it was ninepence a day in a great many instances. The planters, on the other hand, were stern and angry. They began to turn the people off their lands. They threw down the huts the ex-slaves had lived in; they cut down the fruit trees their former labourers had planted. The result of the ill-will on both sides, of the bad feeling on both sides, and of the planters' lack of tact and patience, was that the labourers were estranged from the estates. The people began to buy land of their own. They were helped with money that was sent out by sympathetic people in England. Many of them also squatted on land that belonged to absent proprietors. The planters cried out that they could not get labour, and the sugar estates began to go out of cultivation.

In 1839 Sir Charles Metcalfe succeeded Sir Lionel Smith as Governor. In this same year a drought began which lasted till the Spring of 1841. It caused a great deal of loss and distress.

In 1841 a number of African immigrants arrived to work on the sugar estates. These people were imported to replace the slaves, as the planters contended that it was absolutely necessary to get labour from outside Jamaica. The importation of these Africans was not continued.

In 1842 the Earl of Elgin arrived as Governor.

The General Agricultural Society of Jamaica was founded, and Calabar College was opened.

In 1845 two very important events occurred. The Jamaica Railway, then under a private company, was opened for traffic. The line ran from Kingston to a place called Angels, nearly fifteen miles away.

The first batch of indentured East Indians arrived. After the planters had ceased to import Africans, they turned to India for their labourers.

In 1847 Sir Charles Edward Gray became Governor. The financial condition of the colony was poor, and a year later it became much worse.

In 1848 the British Government adopted the policy of Free Trade. That is, they allowed goods from foreign countries to enter the English market on the same terms as goods from the British colonies; many goods were admitted into England free of duty. In former days, sugar from Cuba had paid a far heavier duty in the English market than the Jamaican. When this advantage was lost, Jamaica could not compete with Cuba and other foreign sugar-producing countries, especially as many of those countries cultivated their estates by means of slave labour.

A crisis occurred in Jamaica. The Planter's Bank which had helped the planters in need of ready money, closed its doors, and the people of the colony declared loudly that the expenses of the Government would have to be reduced. The financial troubles continued for some time, but a still more serious calamity was approaching.

In 1850 Asiatic cholera made its appearance in Jamaica. There was little or no sanitation in the towns of Jamaica at that time. Dwelling houses were often crowded; the yards were kept in a filthy condition; the streets were neglected, and refuse of every description was allowed to rot in them. Water for use in the city and towns was drawn from wells, and was often very impure. Cholera, therefore, found this country an easy victim and 32,000 people died during the epidemic.

In 1852 smallpox broke out in Jamaica. It claimed a large number of victims.

In 1853 Sir Henry Barkly arrived as Governor. He inaugurated a change in the Constitution under which Jamaicans, including Edward Jordan, were appointed to an executive committee. The population had decreased, many estates had gone out of cultivation, the people were poverty-stricken, revenue could not easily be raised and there was no money in the Treasury. The British Government was compelled to lend Jamaica £500,000 to pay off the debts that had accumulated.

In 1857 Captain Charles Darling was appointed Governor of Jamaica. By this time the colony had somewhat recovered from its recent deplorable condition.

In 1858 Jamaican postage stamps were first issued.

In 1859 the telegraph system was introduced into the colony. There were two local riots during this year.

In 1862 General Edward John Eyre became Lieutenant Governor of Jamaica, and in 1864 he was made Governor. The disputes between the planters and the labouring population had grown more bitter and more intense every year since Emancipation. The labourers and their leaders objected to the bringing of East Indian labourers into the country. Since 1861 the American Civil War had been raging, with the result that food imported from America was very dear, and from 1863 a severe drought had begun to afflict the country.

Governor Eyre was not popular. He openly flouted the House of Assembly. While he was still Lieutenant Governor of the colony, a large number of the Jamaican politicians had asked for his recall.

Under his administration, taxes were increased and he himself, early in 1865, described the colony as in a state of degeneration.

Morant Bay Rebellion

In 1865 the Rev. Dr. Underhill, a Baptist minister in England, sent to the Secretary of State for the Colonies a letter on the condition of Jamaica. Dr. Underhill had been in Jamaica and knew the country well. In his letter he complained of the treatment which the lower classes received at the hands of the planters, and urged that certain reforms should be instituted. His letter was sent to General Eyre for the latter's comments. Eyre circulated the letter among the clergymen and Custodes of Jamaica, and nearly all of these denied the assertions of Dr. Underhill.

A copy of the letter found its way into the newspapers. Public meetings, called "Underhill Meetings", were held in different towns, and many of these were presided over by Mr. George William Gordon who was a Member of the House of Assembly. He had once been a Justice of the Peace, but had been deprived of his commission by Eyre who showed an aversion to him because he had exposed certain abuses in the parish of St. Thomas-in-the-East and, in particular, the conduct of the Anglican Rector. Eyre was a strong Anglican and Gordon had become a Baptist.

Gordon made fiery speeches inside and outside the House of Assembly, where from 1864 he represented St. Thomas-in-the-East. He had in St. Thomas a political supporter and religious follower called Paul Bogle who exercised considerable local influence. There were many grievances of which the peasants and labourers of that parish complained; but the Custos, Baron van Kettleholdt, lived in St. Andrew and did not understand what the St. Thomas people felt. He too came to have a strong dislike for Gordon.

George William Gordon

On October 11, when the Vestry was meeting in the Court House at Morant Bay, Paul Bogle and his followers marched into the town and demonstrated in front of the Court House. The volunteer militia, who had been called out by the Custos, fired on the crowd, and Bogle thereupon rushed the volunteers and besieged the Vestry and volunteers in the Court House.

Eventually, Bogle's men set fire to the building, and the Custos and a number of others were killed while trying to escape. Bogle was for a short time master of the parish. But Eyre sent a warship to Morant Bay and poured troops and Maroons into St. Thomas. The resistance was ineffective. Martial Law had been declared and the revolt was put down with terrible severity. The revolt became known as the Morant Bay Rebellion. Over 1,000 huts were burnt; nearly 600 people were shot or hanged and a large number of men and women were flogged. Mr. Gordon was arrested as the instigator of this rebellion, but there was no evidence whatever that he had deliberately instigated it. He was illegally transferred from Kingston, tried by court martial at Morant Bay, found guilty and hanged.

Bogle was captured and hanged. Attempts were made to persuade him to state that Gordon had instigated the revolt, but he persisted in stating that Gordon knew nothing about it.

Paul Bogle

In 1866, early in January, a Royal Commission arrived from England to enquire into the origin and suppression of the rebellion. The English people were very indignant at the severities practised in Jamaica under the Martial Law.

Governor Eyre was suspended, and the head of the Commission, Sir Henry Stokes, became temporary Governor. After thoroughly going into the matter, the Commission found that "the disturbances had their immediate origin in a planned resistance to lawful authority; but that the punishments inflicted during Martial Law were excessive; that the punishment of death was unnecessarily frequent; that the floggings were reckless, and at Bath positively barbarous; and that the burning of 1,000 houses was wanton and cruel." Eyre was then recalled and dismissed from the Imperial Service.

Exercises on Chapter 10

1) What was the effect on Jamaica of Napoleon's defeat at sea? Did Jamaica have to spend a large amount to maintain the soldiers here? Was Jamaica considered a very important military station during the nineteenth century? When did the Jamaican planters begin to complain of poverty?

2) What changes did the Abolition of the Slave Trade bring about in the treatment of the slaves? Were the slaves allowed to earn money by their own efforts?

3) When did the Duke of Manchester arrive? Describe the mutiny that took place in that year. What was the conspiracy that discovered in the following year?

4) When was the Baptist Mission founded? Say what you know about the law that was rescinded in 1816.

5) Give a brief statement of the attitude of the House of Assembly towards the British Government's instructions that the planters should ameliorate the condition of their slaves.

6) When was the Jamaica branch of the Presbyterian Church founded? When was Jamaica made an independent Episcopal See?

7) Give an account of the Christmas Rebellion of 1831 and describe its after-effects.

8) When did the Earl of Mulgrave become Governor? How did the House of Assembly accept his advice that the slaves should be treated more kindly?

9) When was the Abolition Act passed in the British Parliament? What did it decree? How much money did the Jamaica slave-holders receive as compensation for the freeing of their slaves?

10) Describe the Apprenticeship System. Did it work well? On what date did this system cease? Say what you know about the celebration on the August 1, 1838. When was the *Daily Gleaner* first published?

11) What were the relations between the freed people and the planters after Emancipation? Were the people inclined to work with their old masters? What did the planters do? How were the people helped? What began to happen to the sugar estates?

12) When did Sir Charles Metcalfe become Governor? When were African labourers brought into Jamaica? Was this a successful experiment?

13) Describe the two important events that happened in 1845. When did Sir Charles Edward Gray become Governor? Describe the conditions of the colony at that time. Why did Jamaica suffer so severely?

14) When did Asiatic cholera break out in Jamaica? What was the sanitary condition of the country? How many people died during the cholera epidemic? When did smallpox break out in Jamaica?

15) When did General Eyre become Lieutenant Governor? When was he appointed Governor? What were the relationships between the planters and the people of that time? Name two of the causes that inflicted hardships on the people.

16) Was Governor Eyre popular? Who was Dr. Underhill? What were the 'Underhill Meetings'?

17) Who was Mr. George William Gordon? Say what you know about him. What happened on October 11, 1865?

18) Who was Paul Bogle? What took place after the incidents at Morant Bay? Describe the punishment inflicted on many inhabitants of St. Thomas.

19) When did the Royal Commission arrive from England? Why was it sent to Jamaica? Give a brief statement of their report. What happened to Governor Eyre?

JAMAICAN HISTORY PART 4: 1866–1913

CHAPTER 11

CROWN COLONY GOVERNMENT

Immediately after the Morant Bay Rebellion, a great change took place in the Government of the Colony. The House of Assembly agreed to surrender all the rights and privileges it had enjoyed for over two hundred years. It consented that Jamaica should be governed entirely by the British Crown in the future. Since Emancipation, a new situation had arisen. Classes of the population (such as the browns, mixed race and freed slaves) that once had no voice in the Government of the country, had recently been obtaining a large share of political influence. This disgusted the large land-owning class, and the friction between the planters and these people, and between the planters and the Government, had begun making good government impossible.

The roads of the country were neglected. Practically nothing had been done by the Government for education since Emancipation. The workhouses were in a deplorable condition. Very little provision was made for paupers or sick persons who were too poor to pay the heavy doctors' fees charged at the time. Thus the rebellion, though lamentable in itself, nevertheless resulted indirectly in a great deal of good. It brought about a change which gave Jamaica a system of government better suited to deal with the new situation which had arisen since 1838 and gave the colony a period of political rest.

Crown Colony Government

In 1866 Sir John Peter Grant arrived as Jamaica's Governor. He had previously been an administrator in India. He was a very strong and able man, and he at once set about reorganizing the institutions of the colony. A Legislative Council consisting of the Governor, six officials and three non-official members, was appointed by the Crown. A Privy Council was also appointed. Parochial Boards were nominated by the Government. The twenty-two parishes into which the island was then divided were reduced to fourteen. The Police Force was entirely reorganized and District Courts were established. The judges of these courts were officers of the Crown, and it was felt that this change would result in the people obtaining better justice than they had hitherto been able to get.

Immigration (from India) which had been stopped for some time, was now resumed. The Church of England in Jamaica was disestablished, meaning that the Church was no longer the official church of the country. The railway (then owned by a private company) was extended to Old Harbour.

In 1869 nickel coins were first used in Jamaica.

Sir John Peter Grant established a college for the higher education of Jamaican youths and began the Rio Cobre Irrigation Works.

Cablegraphic communication with Europe was established.

In 1871 a census showed the population of the island to be 506,154.

In 1874 Sir John Peter Grant left Jamaica in January. He had effected numerous and far-reaching reforms in every branch of the Public Service. He was one of the best Governors Jamaica ever had.

Sir William Grey arrived as the new Governor.

In 1875 a street car system was started in Kingston by a private company.

In 1877 Sir William Grey left Jamaica and Sir Anthony Musgrave took his place.

In 1879 The Jamaica Railway was purchased by the Government from the company that owned it. The Institute of Jamaica was founded.

In 1880 there was a great hurricane which severely damaged Kingston.

In 1881 the first Jamaica Scholarship was awarded. In that year also occurred the incident which became known as the *Florence* Case.

The *Florence* was a ship on her way from Venezuela to St. Thomas. The Governor, suspicious of her purposes, ordered her detention. A case was brought against him and damages were given against the Governor and his agent to the extent of £6,700.

The British Government instructed the Jamaica Legislative Council to vote the money. The Council refused to do so, on the ground that the Governor had acted in Imperial and not local interests. Rather than do as they were ordered, the Auditor General and Crown Solicitor resigned their seats in the Legislative Council. The Council subsequently voted half the amount asked for, and then the non-official Members resigned.

This led to a strong agitation against the system of Crown Government then in force.

In 1882 a great fire swept over the lower part of Kingston. It destroyed property estimated at £150,000.

In 1883 a Deputation from Jamaica waited on the Secretary of State for the Colonies in England and asked that control over the expenditure of the revenue should be given to the non-official Members of the Legislature. Their representations were favourably received.

During this year Sir Anthony Musgrave left Jamaica and Sir Henry Wylie Norman succeeded him as Governor. Sir Henry Norman brought with him the Order which gave Jamaica a new form of government. Instead of Crown Government pure and simple, there was now to be a Legislative Council, some of whose Members were to be elected on a limited franchise. Arrangements were made for a Government majority of one. But it was decided that the Government should not fill up all its seats, but should let the Elected Members have a majority. The Government, however, retained the right to fill up its vacant seats whenever it thought fit to do so. In this new Legislature the Elected Members were given financial control over Government expenditure.

In 1885 the Railway was extended to Porus and to Ewarton by the Government.

In 1887 there was an outbreak of smallpox.

Marcus Mosiah Garvey, later to be named Jamaica's first National Hero, was born in St. Ann.

In 1888 the old District Courts were abolished and Resident Magistrates' Courts were established in their place.

In 1889 Governor Norman left Jamaica in January. He was one of the most popular Governors Jamaica ever had.

Sir Henry Blake arrived as Governor.

The Legislative Council sold the Jamaica Railway to an American Syndicate.

In 1891 the Jamaica Exhibition was opened by Prince George, who later became King George V. The Exhibition was planned by Sir Henry Blake as a means of advertising Jamaica. Five hotels to accommodate visitors were erected. Over 300,000 persons visited the Exhibition.

Sir Henry Blake formed a Lands Department for the purpose of selling Government land to the peasants on easy terms.

In 1893 elementary education was made free throughout the island.

In 1895 the railway extension to Montego Bay was opened, and the Jamaica Agricultural Society was formed as was the Jamaica Union of Teachers.

In 1896 the Railway extension to Port Antonio was opened.

Sir Henry Blake built many bridges and roads in Jamaica. He thus greatly extended the island's means of communication.

In 1898 Sir Augustus Hemming arrived as Governor. The colony's finances were in a very bad condition. There had been a drought; Jamaican sugar was selling at very low prices abroad; and bananas had not yet become a major export. The Elected Members of the Legislative Council clamoured for a reduction in public expenditure, and eventually the cost of the Government Departments was very much reduced.

The Governor filled up all the vacant seats on the Government side of the Legislative Council. This he did in order to pass a Tariff Bill which he considered of "paramount importance" to the welfare of the colony. Some Elected Members protested, but (with a brief interval) the Government retained a majority of one member in the Legislative Council.

In 1901 an Imperial Direct Line of steamers was inaugurated between Jamaica and England. This represented an attempt on the part of

Mr. Chamberlain, then Secretary of State for the Colonies, to open a market in England for Jamaican bananas. Sir Alfred Jones was head of the shipping arm with which the contract for the direct steamers was made. He was much interested in Jamaica. The Imperial Direct Line operated for ten years.

Queen Victoria died, and Edward VII ascended the throne as King George.

In 1903 a great hurricane swept over the north-eastern section of Jamaica. It did a considerable amount of damage. Sir Augustus Hemming left the colony in 1904, and was succeeded by Sir Alexander Swettenham.

GREAT EARTHQUAKE AND DESTRUCTION OF KINGSTON

In 1907, on January 14, occurred the great earthquake which destroyed the city of Kingston. Three shocks took place within twenty seconds, at about half past three in the afternoon. Every building in Kingston was damaged, and those in the lower part of the city were shattered. The walls fell, killing hundreds of people. Fires started, and soon the commercial area of Kingston was in flames.

About 800 persons lost their lives. Property to the value of £2,000,000 was destroyed. Help was sent from England, the total amount being over a quarter of a million pounds. The Imperial Government lent Jamaica £800,000 to assist in the rebuilding of Kingston. Owing to the prompt assistance which the colony received from the 'mother country', there was no starvation. As quickly as possible, normal conditions were restored. An Assistance Committee, at the head of which, at first, was Dr. Nuttall, Archbishop of the West Indies, did great service in relieving the wants of the people.

One very unfortunate incident occurred. An American squadron steamed into Kingston Harbour shortly after the disaster, and offered assistance. The Admiral landed armed marines without the express sanction of the Governor, who asked that the armed men be withdrawn. The Americans were offended and it was held by the British Government that the Governor had insulted the Admiral. The Governor was told to apologise. This he did, then tendered his resignation. In spite of the efforts of the Colonial Office to induce him to withdraw his resignation, he refused to do so, and in the same year retired into private life.

In 1907, in the month of May, Mr. Sydney (later Baron) Olivier arrived as Governor. He was already well known in the colony. In 1897 he had come to Jamaica as Secretary to a Royal Commission sent to enquire into the condition of the British West Indian Colonies. Later on he returned as a Colonial Secretary, and acted as Governor in 1902, 1903 and 1904. He was called for by the people of Jamaica when it was known that Sir Alexander Swettenham had resigned. He administered the affairs of the colony until January, 1913. Under his guidance a new city arose on the ruins created by the earthquake. He built the chief public buildings on King Street, laid out the public gardens there, built several new roads, reduced taxation, and extended the Jamaica Railway to Clarendon. This Railway had been taken back from the American syndicate in 1900. It had failed to pay its way as a private undertaking. Under Government administration, and owing to the growth of the banana trade, it improved during Sir Sydney Olivier's time.

In 1912, a disastrous hurricane swept over the western parishes in November. After making arrangements for the assistance of the sufferers, the Governor left Jamaica. One of the last acts of his regime was the establishment of Agricultural Loan Banks. Sir Sydney Olivier was a very able and energetic Governor.

In March, 1913 General Sir William Manning arrived as Governor.

Exercises on Chapter 11

1) What was the change in government that took place after the 1865 rebellion? Describe the situation and the general condition of the country which existed since Emancipation.

2) When did Sir John Peter Grant arrive? What sort of Governor was he? State some of the changes and reforms which he instituted. What was the population in 1871?

3) Who became Governor in 1874? When did Sir Anthony Musgrave arrive? For what reason did a deputation go from Jamaica to England in 1883? When did Sir Henry Norman become Governor? What sort of government did he introduce? State the events of the year 1884.

4) When did Sir Henry Blake come to Jamaica? What important transaction took place in the following year? When was the Jamaica Exhibition opened? Why was it planned?

5) Why did Sir Henry Blake form a Lands Department? In what year was elementary education made free? When was the Railway extension to Montego Bay opened? When was the extension to Port Antonio opened?

6) When did Sir Augustus Hemming arrive as Governor? What was the condition of the colony's finances? What was the cause of this state of affairs?

7) When did the Imperial Direct Shipping Line start? Say what you know about it.

8) When did the great Kingston earthquake take place? How many persons were killed? What was the value of property destroyed? Did England help Jamaica then?

9) Say what you know about Sir Sydney Olivier's administration. When did Sir Sydney Olivier leave Jamaica? Who succeeded him?

JAMAICAN HISTORY PART 5: 1914–1962

CHAPTER 12

WORLD WAR I TO 1962 GENERAL ELECTIONS

From 1866 to August, 1914, Jamaica had continued to live in peace and security. During that time the roads of the island were extended and improved. The Railway was greatly extended also; a large number of schools and hospitals were established; and very many of the people acquired land as their own property. Progress was slow but sure. No danger from the outside seemed to threaten the colony. Then suddenly, World War I (also called The Great War) broke out in Europe on August 1, 1914. It involved Jamaica, as it involved every other country in the world, directly or indirectly. Its influence on this island was felt all the time it lasted and the influence of changes it brought about were felt by generations to come.

Jamaica took part in the War, sending to the front about ten thousand men. While the fighting continued Jamaica suffered from a lack of ships to take her products to other countries. This disturbance of trade always takes place in time of war and affects all countries. In the course of time Jamaica was able to resume her regular trade in sugar, rum, tobacco, coffee and cocoa, which were admitted into the English market on better terms than those produced in foreign countries which were not colonies. In other respects also the War brought about many changes in Jamaica, as it did the world over. Many of the soldiers who returned felt that all Jamaicans should play a larger part in the government of their country. This point of view contributed to the development of the movement towards independence. So with the outbreak of World War I began the fifth period of our history.

In 1914 on August 1, Germany plunged Europe into war by declaring war on Russia and next day invading France through Belgium. As England was a party to a treaty with France and Germany to defend Belgium against invasions, England declared war on Germany. It was to be a long and bitter war, lasting four years till 1918. It became known as the Great War and was afterwards called the

First World War, because most nations in the World became involved.

When the war started, Martial Law was immediately proclaimed in Jamaica and a body of troops called the Jamaica Reserve Regiment was formed for the defence of the island. Further, on August 14, a fund was launched which raised £20,000 by year-end to provide comforts for British soldiers.

On September 17, the Legislative Council voted £50,000 to purchase sugar for donation to England.

In 1915, by voluntary effort, Jamaica began to arrange to send soldiers to fight in the Great War. A contingent of 500 men was sent off on November 8. The Legislative Council took over the effort.

On August 12 and 13 a hurricane hit the island; a second occurred on September 25 and 26. Both wrought much damage to property and agriculture, especially to bananas.

In 1916 on January 7, the second contingent of volunteers was sent off to war, with a third following on March 16.

On March 29, the Legislative Council voted £60,000 a year for 40 years as Jamaica's contribution to the expenses of the war. Intensive recruitment started in all parishes. The fourth contingent sailed on September 30. Other West Indian islands followed Jamaica's lead in sending men to fight, so the British War Office resolved to regard all West Indians as one unit to be known as The British West India Regiment.

On August 15 and 16, a hurricane swept Jamaica.

In 1917, on March 6, the Legislative Council introduced compulsory military service, with every male from 16 to 41 years of age being obliged to register. This was to ensure sufficient soldiers being available, but the Conscription Law was never put into effect since all the recruits needed came forward voluntarily. A number of women volunteers also went to England, mainly to join the nursing services.

Five contingents left Jamaica in 1917 bringing the total to nine contingents in all, comprising about 10,000 men.

In May, some women property owners were given the right to vote. The right to vote was formerly given only to male owners of property.

In September, still another hurricane hit the island damaging property, banana plantations and crops. Thus for three successive years the island had not escaped the ravages of hurricanes.

In 1918, May 11, Sir William Manning left Jamaica to go to Ceylon as Governor. In June Sir Leslie Probyn, who had been Governor of Barbados, arrived here as Governor.

On November 1, an Armistice was signed between Germany, Austria, Turkey and Bulgaria on one side and the Allies (chief nations of which were England, France, USA, Italy and Japan) on the other. The war being now practically over, the Jamaican soldiers began to be sent home. The first to return landed in Kingston on May 2, and received a hearty welcome.

Many of the men sent away had died or had been wounded, but most of them had escaped injury. In Palestine especially the West Indian soldiers, most of whom were Jamaicans, had distinguished themselves in fighting the Turks.

In 1923 the parishes of Kingston and St. Andrew were amalgamated. The union came into effect on May 1.

In 1924 Sir Samuel Wilson arrived on September 29 as Governor, succeeding to Sir Leslie Probyn. He remained only nine months, leaving the colony in June, 1925. He subsequently became Under-Secretary of State for the Colonies.

In 1925, in January, a delegation consisting of several members of the British Parliament paid a visit to Jamaica; this was a very important event, for the visitors were influential men and by seeing for themselves were able to carry back to England a better knowledge of Jamaican affairs, both political and economic.

The Hon. A. S. Jelfe, Colonial Secretary, arrived in October and administered the Government until a successor to Sir Samuel Wilson was appointed.

In 1926, in April, Sir Reginald Edward Stubbs arrived as Governor. In May there was held, in a room in the House of Lords (one of the

Houses of Parliament in England), a West Indian Conference. It was attended by representatives of the West Indian colonies and its object was to provide a place where representatives of the different Governments could meet and discuss their problems.

During this year the West India Regiment was disbanded. The Regiment had a long and distinguished career It was first formed in America as the North Carolina Regiment in the year 1779. It was later re-organized and named the West India Regiment. It took part in the capture of St. Lucia, Martinique, Guadeloupe and Dominica, during the Napoleonic Wars. During the latter part of the nineteenth century it was frequently engaged in operations on the West Coast of Africa, notably Ashantee (1873), West Africa (1887, 1892–1894), and Sierra Leone (1898). In World War I (1914–1918) the Regiment saw service in Palestine, the Cameroons and East Africa.

The final parade of the Regiment was held at Up Park Camp on the 26th October, 1926. Later on, in February, 1927, the Colours were taken to England in the charge of several officers. The King received the Colours at Buckingham Palace on February 18. In receiving them, His Majesty said: "I am proud to take charge of the Colours to be preserved and held in remembrance of a great Regiment."

The Band of the Regiment, which always had a great musical reputation, has been kept in existence as a memory. The band members still wear the historic Zouave uniform.

In 1927 on May 4, the Hermitage Dam, on the Wag Water River, was opened. It was built to provide a reserve water supply for the Corporate Area of Kingston and St. Andrew. The dam is 43 metres (142 feet) high; 141.7 metres (465 feet) wide, and is capable of storing 1,627,550,000 litres (430,000,000 gallons) of water. It took two and a half years to build.

In August, an organization called the Jamaica Banana Producers' Association was formed. The object was to unite all the banana growers of the island, or as many of them as possible, in one large company to sell their fruit together. By so doing they hoped to obtain the best prices when the fruit was sold in the markets abroad. A direct line of steamers was to be run as part of the scheme. The Government supported the idea and helped the Association to start operating.

The fruit industry was also further assisted by a line of steamers to Canada. The object was to encourage Canadian and West Indian businessmen to do more business with one another.

1930, in February, a delegation headed by Lord Olivier visited Jamaica to enquire into the state of the sugar industry. Visits were also paid to other West Indian colonies for the same reason. The industry had been receiving support from the British Government in the form of a reduced tax. It was being said that the support should be taken away. The delegation was sent out to find out the exact state of affairs in the different colonies.

In 1932 the Cayman Islands were severely hit by a disastrous hurricane, which swept over them on the night of Tuesday, November 8. In Grand Cayman many buildings were demolished, but there was no loss of life.

The island of Cayman Brac was completely devastated. Dwelling houses and stores were wrecked by wind and sea. Hundreds of the inhabitants were injured, many of the seriously, and 67 lost their lives. In Little Cayman similar damage was done to buildings and many of the inhabitants were injured, but no lives were lost.

On November 9, Sir Edward Stubbs sailed from Jamaica, having completed his term of office, to assume the Governorship of Cyprus. His administration was a very successful one. Stubbs had lent great encouragement to the idea of local enterprise, and important economic developments took place during his administration.

He was succeeded by Sir Ransford Slater, K.C.M.G., C.B.E., who arrived in Jamaica as Governor on November 21.

In 1933, between the night of August 14 and the morning of the 15th, a disastrous flood of record intensity occurred in Kingston and Lower St. Andrew, taking 53 lives and destroying over £300,000 of Government, Municipal and private property. The flood followed very heavy rains which had been falling for several weeks and the swollen gully courses overflowed their banks, taking away houses and drowning the people sleeping in them. Nearly 12.7 cm (5 inches) of rain fell in one hour, and the rainfall for the day was 29.46 cm (11.60 inches). A severe water shortage was caused by the gullies bursting the water mains. Relief measures were carried out and a fund, opened by the Governor, provided nearly £5,000 of aid for the sufferers.

In 1934, on October 24, Sir Edward Denham arrived as Governor, in succession to Sir Ransford Slater, who left Jamaica in April, retiring from the Governorship on the grounds of illhealth.

In 1935, on May 6, King George V celebrated the Silver Jubilee of his reign.

In 1936 King George V died, on January 20, after a short illness. The Prince of Wales ascended the throne as King Edward VIII; he abdicated on December 10.

On the abdication of Edward VIII, his brother the Duke of York, was called to the throne as George VI. He was crowned, with his wife Elizabeth as queen at Westminster Abbey on May 12,1937.

On April 3, a radio-telephone service was inaugurated by which persons in Jamaica were able to speak over the telephone with others in the United States, England, Canada, Mexico and Cuba.

The Jamaica Progressive League first advocated self-government for Jamaica.

1938 Riots

In 1938 discontent over wages and unemployment throughout the island led to the appointment by the Government of a Commission to enquire into the situation. Before the Commission could conclude its work, serious labour disturbances broke out at Frome, Westmoreland, followed by grave disorders in Kingston, St. Mary, St. James and other parts of the island. One of the leaders of the movement, Alexander Bustamante, was arrested but freed afterwards. The first recognized labour union in Jamaica, the Bustamante

Industrial Trade Union was then formed by him. These disturbances, which occurred during the same period as troubles in the other West Indian islands, led the Imperial Government to send out the West India Royal Commission, the Moyne Commission, which took evidence here and in other West Indian territories.

Sir Edward Denham, Governor, died in the Kingston Public Hospital on June 2 and was buried at sea on the following day. He was succeeded by Sir Arthur Richards, who arrived in Jamaica on August 19.

The People's National Party was formed under the leadership of Norman W. Manley on September 18 in the Ward Theatre.

In 1939 an important improvement to internal communications was made with the inauguration of the All-Island Trunk Telephone Service to connect all the principal towns of the island. The first connection was opened to the public on April 1.

In September, the Second World War broke out in Europe, in which Britain became involved. Germany attacked and invaded Poland. Great Britain had a treaty with Poland and so, with the Dominions and Colonies, declared war on Germany. Jamaica, like other parts of the Empire, was immediately placed under the Defence of the Realm Act, under which the Governor made regulations controlling the prices of all commodities to prevent profiteering, controlling foreign exchange, and imposing censorship of the press, mails and of telegraph and cable messages.

In 1940 Great Britain and the United States entered into an arrangement by which the United States was granted air, military and naval bases in British territory. Among the places selected for these bases was Jamaica; Portland Bight was chosen for one and the second was at Vernamfield in Clarendon. A corps of American engineers arrived in the island shortly after the arrangement between the two countries was completed, and immediately set to work.

In 1942, on March 9, the Anglo-American Caribbean Commission was formed. Its object was to co-ordinate efforts in planning agricultural and other research in the Caribbean. The Commission consisted of six members, three appointed by the British Government and three by the USA. Later it was broadened to take in the

French and Dutch West Indies. Members from those governments were appointed and it became the Caribbean Commission.

In June, Marcus Mosiah Garvey died in London.

In 1943, on July 8, the Jamaica Labour Party was founded under the leadership of Alexander Bustamante in the Ward Theatre.

In August, agricultural labourers (sometimes called farm workers) were recruited for temporary employment in the USA to meet wartime needs. So successful was the venture that recruitment was repeated year by year, and the plan extended to other West Indian islands.

In September, Sir John Huggins arrived as Governor in succession to Sir Arthur Richards, who went to Nigeria to assume the Governorship there.

In 1944, on August 20, a disastrous hurricane swept over Jamaica, almost completely destroying the coconut industry. Many homes, as well as schools and other public buildings, were badly damaged and some completely demolished.

On November 20, a new Constitution was proclaimed, under which the island obtained representative, though not responsible government. In place of the single Legislative Council, presided over by the Governor, there was created one wholly-elected body, the House of Representatives, chosen under Universal Adult Suffrage and presided over by its own Speaker; and a Legislative Council, partly ex-officio and partly nominated by the Governor. There also came into existence an Executive Council of ten Members, five chosen by the House of Representatives and five by the Governor. November 20 was declared a public holiday and was known as Constitution Day until after Independence in 1962 when it was replaced by National Heroes Day on the third Monday of October. In the General Elections that followed, the Jamaica Labour Party, led by Alexander Bustamante, obtained a large majority over the People's National Party.

In 1945 the Second World War came to an end. The Germans collapsed in Europe in May, and the Japanese yielded in August after being subjected to intensive bombing, which included the first use of the atomic bomb on Nagasaki and Hiroshima.

In 1947 a conference took place in Montego Bay to consider uniting the British West Indies under a single Federal Government. The subject had been discussed informally from time to time, but this was the first occasion on which representatives of all the British Caribbean peoples met to give the matter official consideration. Representatives were sent by the Governments of all the territories, namely: Jamaica, Trinidad, Barbados, the Windward Islands, the Leeward Islands, British Guiana and British Honduras, and the conference was presided over by the Right Hon. Arthur Creech Jones, Secretary of State for the Colonies. A Standing Committee to study the problem was appointed; it made a report three years later, which was the basis for further debate in all the territories as to the desirability of federation.

In 1948 the University College of the West Indies was founded at Mona, St. Andrew. It received support from the Governments of all the British Caribbean territories.

In August the Jamaica Public Service Co. Ltd., abolished its tramway system in favour of buses for all public transport.

In the first post-war Olympics, held in London, England, Arthur Wint won a gold medal and Herbert McKenley a silver in the 400 metres.

In 1949 new General Elections were held. The Jamaica Labour Party again won, but by a greatly reduced majority in the House of Representatives.

In 1950, on July 9, commercial broadcasting was started by The Jamaica Broadcasting Co. in Kingston. In 1958, the name was changed to Radio Jamaica and Rediffusion Ltd. (RJR).

In 1951 Sir Hugh Mackintosh Foot became Governor in succession to Sir John Huggins.

On August 17, the most severe hurricane in seventy years, Hurricane Charlie, swept over the island. It did great damage in Kingston. Port Royal was destroyed for the third time in its history. Morant Bay was hard hit. The loss of life was in excess of 150.

In 1952, on February 6, King George VI died. His Majesty had been ill for some time and had undergone a serious operation. He was gradually convalescing from this illness when he died, and Princess Elizabeth ascended the throne as Queen Elizabeth II.

The manufacture of cement in Jamaica was started by the Caribbean Cement Company at Rockfort, four miles from Kingston, on the road to St. Thomas.

In May, government set up the Agricultural Development Corporation (often referred to as the ADC) to promote further development of agriculture throughout the island. Early emphasis was on rice-growing. In June, government set up the Industrial Development Corporation, later called the JIDC, to aid expansion in industry and to help to attract overseas capital in setting up industries in the island.

In the Olympics, held in Helsinki, Finland, Jamaica's team of Arthur Wint, Leslie Laing, Herbert McKenley and George Rhoden won the Olympic 4 x 400 metres relay in world record time, as did Rhoden in winning the gold in the 400 metres. McKenley won the silver in the 100 and 400 metres and Wint the silver in the 800.

The Jamaican 4 x 440 yds. relay team at the Olympics in Helsinki, Finland, 1952

In 1953 a broadening of the Constitution was put into effect. The number of Ministries was increased to nine, giving the popular side of the Government a Cabinet for the first time with Ministers responsible for their portfolio, and with the elected Leader becoming Chief Minister. Mr. Alexander Bustamante was the first Chief Minister.

In November, Queen Elizabeth II stopped off for two days on her way to Australia, this being the first time that Jamaica had been visited by a reigning British monarch. Great crowds cheered Her Majesty at many points. She was accompanied by her husband, Prince Philip, Duke of Edinburgh.

In 1954 success attended an Industrial Fair held in Kingston by the Jamaica Manufacturers' Association. In November, President William V. Tubman of Liberia paid a State visit.

In July there was a serious outbreak of poliomyelitis. It was brought under control by December, by which time 759 cases had been reported. There were 94 deaths.

In 1955 island-wide celebrations marked the 300th Anniversary of the coming of Penn and Venables in 1655, and thus the tercentenary of association with Britain. The year opened politically with General Elections in January. The People's National Party gained a majority, and on February 2 Norman W. Manley took office as Chief Minister.

Later, in February, an official goodwill visit to Jamaica was paid by General Paul Magloire, President of Haiti. Less than a week afterwards, HRH Princess Margaret spent five days in Jamaica during the course of her official tour through the British Caribbean. She opened a new hospital at Morant Bay which was named for her.

Then followed Señor Luis Muñoz Marín, Governor of Puerto Rico, who opened the Agricultural Fair at Denbigh. The second Industrial Fair in Kingston was opened in September by the Hon. Adlai Stevenson, former candidate for the Presidency of the United States.

Tercentenary activities which went on for the full year included a "Bandwagon" show which made a circuit of the parishes with artistic and athletic events of all kinds.

In 1956 a conference held in London of representatives of the West Indian island territories settled major points concerning Federation, exclusive of the name of the new nation-to-be and the site of its capital. A Commission of three Englishmen was appointed to tour the region and propose three locations from which the capital would be chosen. Her Majesty Queen Elizabeth II gave her approval on the 23rd February.

Migration to England, which for some years since the Second World War had been rising from almost a trickle, gathered momentum and over 17,000 Jamaicans went to England to seek work in this year.

In 1957, early in the year, a final Federation Conference took place at Mona, St. Andrew. The name West Indies was adopted for the Federation. The Commission on the capital recommended Barbados, Jamaica and Trinidad in the order named. By vote of the regional delegates, Trinidad was selected.

Elaborate naval, military and civic displays attended the unveiling of historical markers at Port Royal, the most important being a plaque in honor of naval heroes who had commanded there. His Excellency the Governor presided.

In January a new system of land valuation for tax purposes was introduced, based on unimproved value instead of an improved value as before. It was planned to introduce this system gradually, to each parish in turn.

On March 1 there was a heavy earthquake which shook almost the entire island, causing substantial damage to buildings.

During this year Government policy on education was revised and expanded whereby 1,500 free places in secondary schools and 50 scholarships and bursaries to the University College of the West Indies were to be granted annually.

In June, the Mona Reservoir in St. Andrew, building of which had started in the early 1940s, was put into service. It has a capacity of 3,122,625,000 litres (825,000,000 gallons).

On November 11, Jamaica received full internal self-government which meant a complete change of the political structure that had existed for almost three centuries. This change gave control of all internal matters to a Council of Ministers called the Executive Council, nominated by the Governor on the recommendation of the Chief Minister, who now became known as Premier. This Parliamentary system was modelled on that of the United Kingdom. There were now ten Ministers instead of the nine under the 1953 Constitution.

Sir Kenneth Blackburne, formerly Governor of the Leeward Islands, arrived on December 18 to take over as Governor from Sir Hugh Foot, who had left the island on November 18 to go to Cyprus as Governor.

During this year bauxite and alumina exports almost doubled those of 1956. Financial arrangements between government and the bauxite companies were revised, whereby government received greatly increased revenues from the mining companies. Migrants to England in this year numbered 13,087.

In 1958 Jamaica became a member territory of the West Indies Federation when it was proclaimed on February 23. During this year the Sugar Industry Labour Welfare Board was established to improve and control the conditions of workers and their dependents on sugar estates and cane farms. In December, Government set up the Jamaica National Trust Commission with power to take steps for the purchase and preservation of National Monuments.

On December 31 the Jamaica Regiment was disbanded, most of its members being absorbed the next day by the West India Regiment.

Migrants to the United Kingdom in this year amounted to 9,992.

In 1959, on March 17, the Hon. Noel Nethersole, Minister of Finance, died suddenly of a heart attack while preparing the Government Budget. In a by-election, Mr. Vernon Arnett replaced him as Member of the House of Representatives (MHR) and Minister of Finance.

In Federal Elections held in April, the Bustamante-led Democratic Labour Party won 12 seats in Jamaica to 5 won by the Federal Labour Party, led by Norman Manley.

On June 14, the Jamaica Broadcasting Corporation, run by a Government Statutory Board, started operations, thus bringing a second broadcasting station to the island.

On July 4, important changes in the Constitution of Jamaica were proclaimed. The Council of Ministers established by the 1957 Constitution was now replaced by a Cabinet with a Premier.

The number of electoral constituencies for electing Members of the House of Representatives was increased from 32 to 45.

The new Montego Bay International Air Terminal was officially opened to traffic on July 9, while in August the new 2,320 metre (7,600 foot) runway at the Palisadoes Airport, near Kingston, was opened to traffic, even though the new terminal building was still under construction.

On July 28 there was a General Election, as a result of which the People's National Party was returned to power, having won 29 seats in the House against the Jamaica Labour Party's 16 seats. Mr. Norman Manley, Q.C., became Premier and assumed the portfolio of Minister of Development. For the first time, a Minister of Home Affairs, responsible for internal security, was appointed.

Work began in this year on the important Negril development project in the west of the island.

Migrants to Britain in this year numbered 12,796.

In 1960, in the course of the year, the Governor, Sir Kenneth Blackburne, went on overseas leave and Mr. Geoffrey Gunter was appointed to act in his place. This was the first occasion on which a Jamaican had been appointed in this way to represent the Crown since the surrender of the old Constitution in 1866. Mr. Gunter was later knighted.

On October 26, the Legislature was transferred from Headquarters House, where it had been located for 88 years, to a new building next door on Duke Street. This new House was named Gordon House in honour of the great Jamaican patriot, George William Gordon, who had been a member of the House of Assembly under the old Constitution and the most distinguished victim of the aftermath of the 1865 Morant Bay rebellion.

During this year considerable expansion of the manufacturing industry took place. New industries appeared, and important amalgamations of businesses and remodelling of factories took place or were completed.

In November the Government awarded 75 bursaries to the University of the West Indies.

Migrants to the United Kingdom reached the figure of 32,060 in this year.

In 1961, in May, the Government opened a national bank, the Bank of Jamaica, thus marking a new and important phase in the development of the island's financial institutions.

On September 19, a Referendum was held for the people of Jamaica to vote as to whether or not they wished the island to remain in the West Indies Federation. 256,261 people voted against and 217,319 people voted for Federation. As a result, Jamaica decided to withdraw from the Federation, which was later dissolved. Jamaica then asked Britain for Independence.

A conference was held in London between Jamaican leaders and the British Government which resulted in the granting of independence with Dominion status to Jamaica on the basis of an agreed Constitution. The agreed date for Independence was set for August 6, 1962.

Migration to the United Kingdom in this year exceeded 39,000.

In 1962, on April 10, a general election was held. The Jamaica Labour Party won 26 seats, while the People's National Party won the remaining 19 seats. The Government therefore passed from the PNP to the JLP and Alexander Bustamante became Prime Minister.

On May 31, the West Indies Federation was dissolved. Jamaica, after her decision of late September, 1961, to secede, had remained a member until the final dissolution. The hope of the Federation continuing without Jamaica was dashed when Premier Eric Williams of Trinidad and Tobago withdrew his country with the statement, "1 from 10 leaves 0".

On June 22, the last British Regiment in Jamaica, the Royal Hampshire Regiment, left the island, thus bringing to a close an era which had begun in 1655, since when British troops had always been quartered in Jamaica.

Exercises on Chapter 12

1) When did the Great War begin? What part did Jamaica play? On what date was the war brought to a close?

2) In what year did some women in Jamaica get the right to vote?

3) What was the date of the amalgamation of the parishes of Kingston and St. Andrew?

4) When was (a) the Hermitage Dam opened? (b) the Mona Reservoir put into service?

5) In what year was the Jamaica Banana Producers' Association formed? What was its objective?

6) In what year did a disastrous flood of record intensity hit Kingston and lower St. Andrew? How many lives were lost? What was the value of destruction to property, both Government's and the private sector?

7) When was self-government for Jamaica first advocated? By whom?

8) Relate briefly what events took place in Jamaica in respect of labour unrest in 1938.

9) When was the first labour union formed and by whom?

10) In which year was the People's National Party formed and under whose leadership?

11) Give the years associated with the following:

   (a) The All-Island Trunk Telephone Service.

   (b) First recruitment for farm labour in the USA.

   (c) The founding of the University College of the West Indies.

   (d) The tramcars in Kingston giving way to buses.

   (e) The start of commercial broadcasting in Jamaica.

(f) The start of the manufacturing of cement in Jamaica.

12) When was Universal Adult Suffrage introduced into Jamaica? What did it provide?

13) Who was the first reigning English Monarch to visit Jamaica? When? Who accompanied the Monarch? How long did the visit last?

14) In what year, and on what date did Jamaica become a member territory of the West Indies Federation? When did Jamaica withdraw? How was this withdrawal decided?

15) On what date did Jamaica get full internal self-government? What was the title of the head of the ruling elected Party before and after this event?

16) In what year was the Legislature transferred from Headquarters House to Gordon House? For whom was Gordon House named? Where is it located?

17) Which political parties won the General Elections in 1944? 1949? 1955? 1959? 1962?

CHAPTER 13

POST-INDEPENDENCE 1962–1972

At midnight on August 5, 1962, Jamaica became a free independent nation within the British Commonwealth of Nations. A ceremony marking the event was held at the newly constructed National Stadium in Kingston, which was filled to its capacity of 35,000. The chief persons taking part were Her Royal Highness Princess Margaret (representing Her Majesty Queen Elizabeth II); her husband, the Earl of Snowdon; Sir Kenneth Blackburne, who had been nominated by the Queen on the recommendation of our then Premier to be Jamaica's first Governor-General; Sir Alexander Bustamante, Jamaica's first Prime Minister; and Mr. Norman Manley, Leader of the Opposition. Prayers were offered by the Rt. Rev. Percival Gibson, Lord Bishop of Jamaica; His Lordship Bishop McEleney, Roman Catholic Bishop of Kingston; Bishop S. U. Hastings, Chairman of the Jamaica Christian Council; Mr. Ernest H. DaSouza, Jr., as acting spiritual leader of the Jewish Community.

Rt. Excellent Sir Alexander Bustamante, Jamaica's first Prime Minister

Hundreds of notable guests and visitors from many countries of the world attended, among them Mr. Lyndon Johnson, Vice-President of the United States of America, as the personal representative of President John Kennedy.

Precisely at midnight, August 5, the Union Jack – the British flag – was lowered and the Jamaican flag hoisted. The new National Anthem of Jamaica was sung by combined choirs. This was followed by a magnificent fireworks display at the Stadium. In other parts of the Corporate Area, and in the country parishes, there were also displays of fireworks.

There followed two Public Holidays which were given overt great rejoicing throughout the island. Kingston, the capital, and all other parish capitals were gaily decorated with flags and bunting, and highly illuminated at nights. There were many civic and social events and there was public dancing in the streets.

When the dust of the Independence celebrations had disappeared, Jamaica settled down to the business of establishing herself as one of the nations of the world.

The drive to expand industry was considerably intensified. A new emphasis was placed on agricultural expansion. All this became more urgent in view of the slowing down of migration to the United Kingdom, which brought with it the necessity of providing gainful employment for Jamaica's increasing population.

In the wake of this came the further obligation of spreading education wider so as to equip the people with skills and trades to enable them to keep pace with advancements in the outside world.

Although involved with the immediate problems of a new nation, Jamaica looked back into her past and sought to pay homage to men who had played a great part in the progression to independence.

The George VI Memorial Park became the National Heroes' Park. There the National Shrine was erected and three illustrious Sons of Jamaica, Marcus Mosiah Garvey, Paul Bogle and George William Gordon, were enshrined. A special site was provided as the final resting place of Jamaican Prime Ministers. Sir Donald Sangster was the first Prime Minister to be buried there.

Rt. Excellent Norman Manley, Q.C., first Leader of the Opposition of Independent Jamaica.

In 1962 on August 7, the first meeting of Jamaica's new Parliament was held in Gordon House. H.R.H. Princess Margaret, representing the Queen, opened the session and welcomed Jamaica into the Commonwealth of Nations.

On August 11, the 9th Central American and Caribbean Games opened at the National Stadium. The Games continued until August 25, during which time Jamaica was host to athletes from 14 countries. Jamaican athletes distinguished themselves, winning many gold, silver and bronze medals.

Jamaica was admitted to membership of the United Nations on September 18, the island's first Representative being His Excellency, Mr. Egerton R. Richardson, C.M.G., a Jamaican who had formerly been Financial Secretary of the island.

Jamaica's Representatives at our overseas Missions were appointed, as follows: Ambassador to the United States of America – His Excellency, Mr. Neville N. Ashenheim, C.B.E. (who was knighted on January 1, 1963); High Commissioner to Canada – His Excellency, Mr. E. A. Maynier, O.B.E.; High Commissioner to the United Kingdom – His Excellency, Mr. H. L. Lint, C.M.G. and Consul-General in New York, the United States – Mr. Keith Johnson.

Sir Kenneth Blackburne,
Jamaica's first Governor-
General.

Sir Kenneth Blackburne, last of the British Governors, who had become Governor-General on August 6, left the island on November 30. His place was taken by Senator Clifford Campbell, who was nominated by the Queen on the recommendation of the Prime Minister to be Jamaica's first native Governor-General. Senator Campbell was immediately knighted by the Queen and became Sir Clifford Campbell, G.C.M.G. He took up office on December 1 and moved into residence at King's House on the same day.

Sir Clifford Campbell,
Jamaica's first native Governor-
General, 1962–1973.

In 1963, on March 11, the Hon. Donald Sangster, Minister of Finance, was appointed Deputy Prime Minister.

In July, Mrs. Muriel Carnegie, the first woman to hold such office, was appointed by the Governor-General to serve as Custos Rotulorum for the parish of Westmoreland.

Between October 5 and 7, Jamaica was ravaged by flood rains from Hurricane Flora which passed to the north of the island and settled over Cuba for three to four days. The Corporate Area endured the heaviest rainfall of the century. Damage to the island was estimated at £2 million.

In November, Miss Carol Joan Crawford was chosen "Miss World 1963" from thirty-nine contestants in London. This was the first time that a Jamaican had ever been awarded this title.

In December, the United Nations accepted a Jamaican resolution that 1968 should be observed as the International Year of Human Rights.

On December 11, the House of Representatives passed a Bill amending the Representation of the People Law to make provision for the new Finger-Print and Photograph Voter Registration.

Late in December, a Bank of Jamaica survey showed that £12 million was in circulation in the island, more money than there had ever been in the history of Jamaica.

Sir Alexander Bustamante was appointed a member of the Privy Council of England in the Queen's New Year's Honours List.

In 1964, the three hundredth anniversary of the introduction of the Parliamentary form of government into Jamaica was celebrated.

In January, a United Kingdom Parliamentary delegation presented the House of Representatives with a Speaker's Chair, the Independence gift from the British House of Commons.

The Kingston Oil Refinery of Esso West Indies Ltd. on Marcus Garvey Drive, went into operation on March 5.

On March 18, the Government dissolved the Portland Parish Council a period of two years and appointed a Commissioner to exercise the powers and duties of the Council during that time.

Government dissolved the Kingston and St. Andrew Corporation Council on June 23 and two Commissioners were appointed to administer the affairs of the Corporate Area.

The Hon. Kenneth Jones, Minister of Communications and Works, died in the Montego Bay Hospital on October 11 from injuries he received when he fell from a balcony at the Sunset Lodge Hotel, Montego Bay.

Jamaica's first National Hero, Marcus Garvey, was enshrined in State and Church ceremonies at King George VI Memorial Park, on November 15. His body was brought home from the Kendal Green cemetery in London, England, where he had been buried on his death in June 1940.

Rt. Excellent Marcus Mosiah Garvey, Jamaica's first National Hero

On November 16, the Tenth Conference of the Commonwealth Parliamentary Association was opened in the General Assembly Hall at the University of the West Indies by the Hon. Donald Sangster, Deputy Prime Minister and Minister of Finance. Mr. Sangster, President of the Association for the year, presided over the Conference.

1965 in January, Jamaica became a member of the United Nations Human Rights Commission for the first time.

The National Volunteers Organization, an organization for voluntary social service, was established in June.

Dr. Martin Luther King, Jnr., Nobel Peace Prize winner and United States Civil Rights Leader, delivered the valedictory address for graduating students of the University of the West Indies on June 20. On the following day, Dr. King was presented with the Keys to the City of Kingston at a civic reception at the National Stadium.

The 100th Anniversary of the Morant Bay Rebellion was celebrated in this year. On October 11, at a ceremony in Morant Bay, the burial spot for hundreds of victims of the harshness of Governor John Eyre, was consecrated. The Acting Prime Minister unveiled a statue of Paul Bogle, sculpted by Mrs. Edna Manley, in front of the Morant Bay Court House. It was announced that in honour of Bogle, a son of St. Thomas, the town of Morant Bay would be raised to mayoral Status.

The climax of the 1865 Centenary celebrations came at the National Shrine, George VI Memorial Park, on October 24, when a monument honouring Paul Bogle and George William Gordon was dedicated to their memory. The ceremony at the National Shrine followed a State Memorial Service for Bogle and Gordon, held in the East Queen Street Baptist Church in Kingston.

On November 28, the first Canadian Prime Minister in office to visit Jamaica, the Rt. Hon. Lester B. Pearson, arrived in the island for discussions with the Acting Prime Minister, the Hon. Donald Sangster, on matters of common interest.

In 1966 in March, Her Majesty Queen Elizabeth II, accompanied by her husband, HRH Prince Philip, Duke of Edinburgh, arrived in Jamaica for a four-day visit. Thousands of people lined the sweets to greet Queen Elizabeth, who was visiting the island for the first time in thirteen years. On March 4, the Queen opened the 1966/67 Session of the Jamaican Parliament.

On April 21, His Imperial Majesty Haile Selassie I, Emperor of Ethiopia, King of Kings, Conquering Lion of Judah, arrived in Jamaica for a three-day state visit. He received an overwhelming welcome especially from members of the Rastafarian faith. H.I.M.

Haile Selassie I addressed Members of both Houses of the Jamaican Parliament and, at a special ceremony at the University of the West Indies, received the honorary degree of Doctor of Laws.

The Rt. Reverend Samuel Carter, S.J., was consecrated Auxiliary Roman Catholic Bishop of Kingston with the Titular

H.I.M. Haile Selassie I, Emperor of Ethiopia.

See of Cenculliana, at the Holy Trinity Cathedral on April 25. Bishop Carter was the first Jamaican-born Roman Catholic Bishop.

A ceremony marking the inauguration of Air Jamaica was held at the Palisadoes Airport on May 1, coinciding with the departure of the first Air Jamaica flight to Miami.

In June, the Government entered into an agreement with Messrs. Montego Freeport Ltd. by which the company would undertake a 5,000-acre land reclamation and development project in the Bogue Islands area of Montego Bay at the cost of £3 million.

The Portland Parish Council which was dissolved in 1963, came into existence again in July, when Councillors elected in the June Island Parochial Elections, were sworn m.

On July 30, the 5,000-seat National Arena adjoining the National Stadium was opened by the Acting Prime Minister, the Hon. Donald Sangster.

HRH Prince Philip, Duke of Edinburgh, who arrived in Jamaica on August 3, with his two elder children, Prince Charles and Princess Anne, officially opened the eighth British Empire and Commonwealth Games on the night of August 4. The Duke read the Queen's Message to the Games at a colourful Opening Ceremony in the National Stadium. A total of 1,500 athletes from thirty-five Commonwealth countries competed in the Games which ended on August 13.

On August 15, Prince Philip opened the 2nd Commonwealth Paraplegic Games at the University's playing fields, Mona. Prince Philip, Prince Charles and Princess Anne left the island on August 16, ending their thirteen-day visit.

In September the House of Representatives decided to increase the number of seats in the House from 45 to 53.

At midnight on Sunday, October 2, a State of Emergency was declared in Western Kingston. The Declaration of the State of Emergency was pronounced by the Minister of Home Affairs, the Hon. Roy McNeil, after discussions with the Prime Minister, Sir Alexander Bustamante, and advisers at Jamaica House. The Emergency was a direct result of a new outburst of the political gang violence in the area, which over the preceding three months had resulted in six deaths. Police and military personnel cordoned off the troubled zone and a curfew from 10 p.m. to 6 a.m. was imposed. The State of Emergency was declared ended November 4.

On November 20, President Kenneth Kaunda of Zambia arrived in Jamaica for a three-day official visit, part of a Caribbean and Western Hemisphere tour. He was presented with the Keys to the City of Kingston and a souvenir copy of the history of the city on his arrival at the Palisadoes Airport.

Dr. Kaunda addressed a special joint sitting of the Jamaican Parliament on November 22.

The Government announced, on December 13, the start of an £8 million development programme for education over the next three years. Seven million pounds sterling were to be spent on building fifty junior secondary schools, expanding facilities for teacher-training and the College of Arts, Science and Technology as well as the Jamaica School of Agriculture. The other £1 million was to be used in the provision of primary schools and teachers' cottages. Half of the sum would be provided by the Jamaican Government and the other half by a loan from the Canadian Government.

In 1967, in January, the Acting Prime Minister, The Hon. Donald Sangster announced the formation of a new bank, the Jamaica Citizens Bank Ltd. with a capitalization of £2 million. The Bank would be owned 51% in Jamaica and 49% in Atlanta, Georgia, and would be the first local bank established since the ill-fated Sterling Bank of several decades earlier.

Parliament was dissolved on January 24 and General Elections were held on February 21. The Jamaica Labour Party, which had been in power for the preceding five years, again emerged victorious, winning 33 seats to the People's National Party's 20.

On February 23, the Hon. Donald Sangster, First Deputy Leader of the Labour Party, was sworn in by the Governor-General, Sir Clifford Campbell, as Prime Minister of Jamaica.

**Rt. Hon. Sir Donald Sangster,
Prime Minister of Jamaica,
1967.**

Sir Neville Ashenheim, Jamaica's first Ambassador to the United States, resigned his position in March.

Sir Donald Sangster, 55, Jamaica's second Prime Minister, died on April 11 in the Montreal Neurological Institute, Canada, where his strong constitution had been fighting a losing battle against brain haemorrhage since March 21 when he was flown to Montreal for specialist treatment.

On his death-bed, the Prime Minister was created a Knight Commander of the Royal Victorian Order by Her Majesty the Queen.

Rt. Hon. Hugh Shearer, Prime Minister of Jamaica, 1967–1972.

Four hours after the sad news reached Jamaica, the Hon. Hugh Lawson Shearer was sworn in as the third Prime Minister of Jamaica by the Governor-General, Sir Clifford Campbell.

Sir Donald's body was flown home to Jamaica and lay in state at Mountainside, Chapelton and Kingston. On April 17, after a State Funeral Service at the Kingston Parish Church, Sir Donald Sangster was given a hero's burial in the George VI Memorial Park.

In June, Prime Minister Hugh Shearer announced major changes in Departments controlled by some of the Ministries of Government. The Ministry of Finance became the Ministry of Finance and Planning. The Ministry of Development and Welfare became the Ministry of Youth and Development and a new Ministry was created, the Ministry of Legal Affairs.

In the January – June period of this year the average rainfall in the catchment area of the Corporate Area of Kingston and St. Andrew was 170 cm. (66.93 inches), the lowest single figure for the past 25 years. Figures since 1942 showed an average rainfall of 348.66 cm (137.27 inches) in the corresponding periods.

On July 1, the Financial Secretary, the Hon. G. Arthur Brown. became Governor of the Bank of Jamaica. Mr. Brown was also appointed Economic Adviser to the Government.

On July 30, Jamaica signed the "Kennedy Round" Agreement, providing for tariff cuts for industrial products.

The Rt. Rev. Percival W. Gibson, C.B.E., D.D., the first Jamaican to be elevated to the office of Anglican Bishop of Jamaica, retired from that office in September.

Jamaica's steel mill, owned by the Caribbean Steel Company Ltd., Spanish Town, started full scale manufacture and sale of bars in October.

On November 21, the Jamaican £1 was devalued, following a UK devaluation, to a new parity of Ja.£1 to US$2.40.

On November 30, His Grace the Most Rev. John J. McEleney, S.J., D.D., was installed as Archbishop of Kingston in the Holy Trinity Roman Catholic Cathedral, North Street, Kingston, followed by the Consecration of the Rev. Edgerton R. Clarke, D.D., as Bishop of Montego Bay, which now became a Cathedral city. Bishop Clarke was enthroned at the Blessed Sacrament Cathedral, Montego Bay, on December 8.

In 1968, following the inauguration of the Downtown Kingston rebuilding plan, demolition began in mid-February, and the first phase of construction work started in March.

The Rt. Rev. John C. Swaby was enthroned as Anglican Bishop of Jamaica at the Cathedral of St. Jago de la Vega (St. James's Cathedral), Spanish Town, on February 19.

On April 1, the first series of National Development Bonds was issued, free of income tax on the interest.

The opening of Montego Bay's first deep-water pier at Bogue took place on July 28.

Jamaica officially became a member of the Caribbean Free Trade Agreement (CARIFTA) on August 1.

In the last week of August, an island-wide epidemic of "sickness" by members of the Jamaica Constabulary Force, following a threat by policemen to take "positive action", resulted in the Military being called out to maintain order and security. The crisis was due to a dispute over salaries.

An exclusion order effected on October 15 against Dr. Walter Rodney, a Guyanese and Lecturer in African History at the University of the West Indies, led to a demonstration the following day by some students and Faculty members of the University. Civil disorder ensued when hooligan elements took charge and did extensive damage in many parts of the city, estimated at over £1 million. One death was reported.

A National Lottery was established on December 7, when the first draw took place.

The Marcus Garvey Prize for Human Rights (£5,000), awarded posthumously to Dr. Martin Luther King, Jnr., was presented in Jamaica to his widow, Mrs. Coretta Kingston December 10.

The International Sugar Agreement, to which Jamaica was a party and which the Hon. Robert Lightbourne, Minister of Trade and Industry, was largely instrumental in bringing to a conclusion, was signed in Geneva on October 23, and ratified in New York between December 3 and 24. It came into effect on January 1, 1969.

In 1969, the Ministry of Agriculture and Lands was replaced by the Ministry of Agriculture and Fisheries and the Ministry of Rural Land Development. The Minister of Rural Land Development, Mr. W. G. McLaren, was sworn in on January 4, 1969.

Norman Washington Manley, Leader of the Opposition, resigned as such, and later from the House of Representatives, during February, 1969. His son Michael was elected P.N.P. leader, and hence leader of the Parliamentary Opposition, in his place.

The 100th Archbishop of Canterbury, Dr. Michael Ramsay, began his visit to Jamaica, the first by a Primate of England, on March 2.

Air Jamaica (1968) Ltd. was formed between the Government of Jamaica and Air Canada to operate Jamaica's National Airline. Registered in October, 1968, it started operating on April 1, 1969. It replaced Air Jamaica Ltd. which concluded operations on March 31, 1969.

On April 15, Jamaica became a signatory to the Nonproliferation of Nuclear Weapons Treaty.

Jamaica's largest alumina plant, erected by a consortium called Alumina Partners of Jamaica (ALPART) at Nain in St. Elizabeth went into operation on May 18.

The establishment of Jamaica's first merchant bank was announced by the Minister of Finance and Planning on June 26.

The Gleaner Company Ltd. occupied its new plant and offices at 7 North Street, Kingston, in mid-July.

Jamaica's application for membership in the Organization of American States (OAS) was accepted on June 25 and the Charter was signed on June 27. It was approved by the House of Representatives on August 6.

A Student Loan Fund was set up to assist students at tertiary institutions.

Jamaica's own National Honours were established by the National Honours and Awards Act, assented to by the Governor General on July 18.

The death of Norman Washington Manley occurred on September 2. After a State Funeral on September 7, he was buried in the National Shrine area of the King George VI Park.

The change from Jamaican pounds, shillings and pence to decimal currency took place on September 8.

The national holiday for the Queen's Birthday was discontinued and, in its place, National Heroes Day was established on October 20, to be celebrated on the third Monday in October each year thereafter. The first National Heroes to be designated and given the title 'the Right Excellent' were Paul Bogle, George William Gordon, Marcus Mosiah Garvey, Norman Washington Manley (all deceased), and Sir William Alexander Bustamante.

The Charter of the Caribbean Development Bank was signed by representatives of all eighteen member-territories at the Sheraton-Kingston Hotel on October 18.

On October 21, the Jamaican Government and that of the United States of America concluded an Air Transport Agreement allowing for the expansion of commercial air services between the two countries.

Jamaica became a member of the Inter-American Development Bank on December 30, 1969.

In 1970 a symbolic opening of the cross-harbour causeway was performed on January 21, when the Hon. Edward Seaga travelled across it on a tour of the area; however, traffic had started using it before that date.

The Life of Jamaica Insurance Company was established on March 12.

The Rt. Rev. Percival W. Gibson, C.B.E., D.D., retired Anglican Bishop of Jamaica, died at the Nuttall Memorial Hospital, Kingston, on April 3, at the age of 77 after a short illness.

The statue of the Rt. Excellent Sir Alexander Bustamante, sculpted by Alvin Marriott, was unveiled by Lady Bustamante, during a ceremony at the southern end of the Victoria Park on May 24.

Statue of Rt. Excellent Alexander Bustamante

In September, the Rt. Rev. Samuel E. Carter, Roman Catholic Auxiliary Bishop of Kingston, was named to succeed the Most Rev. Joh J. McEleney, who was to resign as Archbishop of Kingston, on November 13.

Twenty-seven Jamaicans were honoured in the first list of Jamaican honours and awards (other than that of National Hero) issued on October 17. Heading the list was the Hon. Robert Lightbourne, Minister of Trade and Industry, who was given the Order of Jamaica, the third highest Jamaican honour. The National Unit Trust was established on October 26.

The first scheduled flight of a Pan-American Jumbo jet to Jamaica took place on November 25.

The opening of the Third World Netball Tournament at the National Stadium took place on December 30.

In 1971, the second Archbishop of Kingston and the first Jamaican to head the Roman Catholic Church in Jamaica, the Most Rev. Samuel E. Carter, S.J., C.D., D.D., was installed at the Holy Trinity Cathedral, Kingston, on February 5.

The First National City Bank of Chicago (Ja) Ltd., opened for business at the Bernard Sunley Building on January 5. The banking hall was officially opened on March 1.

The Prices Commission was officially launched on January 6. The United States hospital ship *Hope* arrived at No. 2 Pier, Kingston, Jamaica, on January 13.

"Tom Cringle's" famous cotton tree near the Ferry Inn on the Spanish Town Road, reputed to be more than two hundred years old, collapsed on February 18.

Jamaica International Telecommunications Limited (JAMINTEL) went into operation on April 1, 1971. The agreement by which the Government of Jamaica became associated with Cable and Wireless in ownership and operation of this company had been signed by the Minister of Communications and Works, the Hon. Cleve Lewis, and the Chairman of Cable and Wireless, Colonel Donald MacMillan, on November 6.

Acquisition by the Government of Jamaica of over 60,000 acres of land from the West Indies Sugar Company Ltd. was ratified by the formal signing of the purchase agreement between the Government and the Company on May 21.

A contract aimed at developing a National Airport Plan to meet aviation needs for the next 20 years was signed between the Ministry of Communications and Works and a Canadian Consulting Group, comprising the Montreal Engineering Company Ltd. and Kates, Peat, Marwick and Company on June 8.

Statue of Rt. Excellent Norman W. Manley

A statue of the Rt. Excellent Norman W. Manley, the work of Alvin Marriott, was unveiled by his widow, Mrs Edna Manley, at the northern end of Victoria Park on July 4.

President Jose Figueres of Costa Rica arrived in Jamaica for an official visit on July 31.

All foreign currencies, including sterling, were placed under Exchange Control on September 6.

"National Heroes" Day was celebrated on October 18 with a military parade and the first investiture of the new Jamaican Awards at Up Park Camp. The Right Excellent Sir Alexander Bustamante received his Order of National Hero insignia from the Governor-General, Sir Clifford Campbell, G.C.M.G.

The Jamaican dollar was revalued on December 28, thus keeping parity with the pound sterling (J$2 = £1) following the devaluation of the United States dollar.

Exercises on Chapter 13

1) Which political party won the general elections in 1962.

2) Who represented the Queen at our Independence Celebrations?

3) Who were Jamaica's first Prime Minister and first Governor General?

4) Who was Jamaica's first native Governor-General? Where did he live?

5) When was the K.S.A.C. Council dissolved?

6) Who was Jamaica's first National Hero? Where is his body now buried?

7) In what year was the 100th anniversary of the Morant Bay Rebellion celebrated?

8) In what way was the town of Morant Bay honoured to mark this occasion? Who were the two patriots honoured in the ceremony?

9) What political party won the General Elections in April, 1962? Who was leader of the party? What did he become?

10) What important visitors came to Jamaica in 1965? 1966?

11) When was the first Air Jamaica flight?

12) Where is the National Arena? When was it opened?

13) What important event took place at the National Stadium from August 4 to 13, 1966?

14) Why was a State of Emergency declared in Western Kingston?

15) Which party won the 1967 General Elections? Who was sworn in as Prime Minister?

16) Who was sworn in as the third Prime Minister of Jamaica?

17) In what year after Independence was the Jamaican currency devalued?

18) Who was awarded the Marcus Garvey Prize for Human Rights and when?

19) Which Minister of the Jamaican Government was instrumental in bringing to a conclusion the International Sugar Agreement of 1968?

20) When did the Rt. Excellent Norman W. Manley die? Where was he buried?

21) On what date did the change-over to decimal currency take place?

22) In what year was the celebration of the Queen's Birthday discontinued? What holiday was substituted for it?

23) Who succeeded Norman Washington Manley as Leader of the People's National Party and Leader of the Opposition in Parliament?

24) When did the famous "Tom Cringle's" cotton tree collapse?

25) When did JAMINTEL (Jamaica International Telecommunications Ltd.) begin its operations?

26) On what occasion did Sir Alexander Bustamante receive the insignia of his Order of National Hero?

JAMAICA HISTORY PART 6 (CONT'D): 1962–1993

CHAPTER 14

POST-INDEPENDENCE 1972–1983

The period 1972–1983 may be characterized as the period of the first full-scale ideological battle the country has ever seen. In 1974, the People's National Party (PNP) declared that "Democratic Socialism" was the new political philosophy for Jamaica. This was dubbed "Communism" by some, partly because of the leader's close friendship with Fidel Castro of Cuba and partly because the PNP was covertly supported by the Workers' Party of Jamaica (a Communist Party). In 1979, the Jamaica Labour Party (JLP) declared itself a "Social Democratic Party" in contradistinction to the PNP.

In March 1980, the PNP Government decided that it should continue efforts to finalize a standby agreement with the International Monetary Fund and was bitterly criticized for this.

The run-up to the General Elections of 1980 was marked by extreme violence in which modern automatic weapons were used and hundreds of people slain.

In 1980, the Jamaica Labour Party under its banner of Nationalism swept the polls, winning 51 seats to the PNP's 9 seats.

The country settled down to a clear accommodation with the United States of America from which it received much financial aid.

In 1972 Parliament was dissolved on February 5 and General Elections were called for February 29. The PNP government was returned to office with 37 seats as against 16 for the JLP in Opposition.

The first Test Match of New Zealand's first tour of the West Indies ended on February 22 in a draw at Sabina Park. The Jamaican, Lawrence Rowe, set a record as the first batsman to score centuries in both innings on his Test debut: 214 and 100 not out.

Rt. Hon. Michael Manley,
Prime Minister of Jamaica
1972–1980, 1989–1992.

Mr. Michael Manley was sworn in on March 2 as Jamaica's fourth Prime Minister, by the Governor-General, Sir Clifford Campbell, at King's House.

The Hon. Robert Lightbourne, O.J., resigned from the Jamaica Labour Party on March 5, to sit as an independent member in the House of Representatives.

Thirteen PNP Senators were named to the Senate on March 17: eight Opposition Senators were named on March 18.

The Opposition boycotted the Opening of Parliament at Gordon House on March 21.

The Centenary celebrations of the City of Kingston as the capital of Jamaica opened on April 9, with Divine Service at Kingston Parish Church. In April there was a tree-planting ceremony. Trees were planted by the Governor-General, the Prime Minister and the Mayor of Kingston.

A National Bauxite Commission, under the chairmanship of Mr. Meyer Matalon, was set up on April 19 to review the conditions of Jamaica's bauxite/alumina industry.

The Rt. Rev. Herbert DaCosta Edmondson, M.A., B.D. of the Anglican Church was consecrated Bishop Suffragan of Mandeville at St. James Cathedral, Spanish Town, on April 25.

The newly-established Revenue Court held its first session at Camp Road on May 18.

The Hon. Michael Manley became Jamaica's second Prime Minister in office to get married when, on June 11, he took as his bride Miss Beverly Anderson, 27-year-old radio and television personality, in a private ceremony performed by the Rev. Ashley A. Smith at the residence of Mr. Manley's mother, Mrs. Edna Manley.

A Jamaican Government Trade Mission, led by Mr. Carlton Alexander, left on June 18 on a visit to European and Asian states, including Russia and the People's Republic of China.

On June 27, Jamaica floated her dollar to retain its existing parity with the pound sterling.

In 1973, on February 28, Sir Clifford Campbell, K.C.V.O., G.C.M.G., retired from the office of Governor-General. Sir Herbert Duffus, Chief Justice, was appointed to act as Governor-General, and he and Lady Duffus took up residence at King's House.

In May, the Government announced Free Education. No tuition fees were to be paid in government Secondary Schools and school services such as games, home economics, drama classes would be free of cost as from September 1974. There was to be free tuition for all Jamaicans admitted to the University of the West Indies.

On June 1, the Hon. Florizel A. Glasspole, C.D., Minister of Education, resigned as Member of Parliament for East Kingston in preparation for being sworn in as Governor-General.

In June, Jamaica received US$29 million in International Monetary Fund (IMF) aid.

The Hon. Eli Matalon resigned on June 8 as Minister of State for Education to contest the by-election in East Kingston to fill the vacancy created by the resignation of the Hon. F. A.Glasspole.

On June 27, the Hon. Florizel A. Glasspole, C.D., was sworn in as Governor-General of Jamaica (the third since Jamaica became independent in 1962) by Sir Herbert Duffus, acting Governor-General at a colourful ceremony at King's House in the presence of a large and distinguished gathering.

The Most Honourable Sir
Florizel Glasspole, Governor-
General of Jamaica 1973–1991

Mr. Matalon won the by-election held on July 3 and was sworn in as Minister of Education, on July 5.

In 1974 the Hon. Chief Leabus Johnothan, Prime Minister of Lesotho paid a five-day state visit to Jamaica in May.

In June a levy imposed a higher royalty for bauxite mined in Jamaica on the bauxite companies. The royalties were to increase in two stages to 8% by 1976/77. On June 27, a million dollars was paid to the government of Jamaica by the bauxite companies.

On September 14, President Julius Nyerere of Tanzania paid a four-day official visit to Jamaica.

In November, Democratic Socialism was formally declared to be the new political philosophy of Jamaica.

In 1975, on January 3, Miss Carmen Parris was appointed Ambassador to France. She was the first woman to be appointed Ambassador by Jamaica.

Rt. Excellent Nanny of the Maroons

In October, Nanny of the Maroons and Samuel Sharpe were declared National Heroes, bringing the number of Jamaican National Heroes to seven. Charles Square in Montego Bay was renamed Sam Sharpe Square after the National Hero.

Rt. Excellent Sam Sharpe.

In November an amendment to the Jamaican Constitution was passed to allow a maximum of four Cabinet Ministers to be appointed from the Senate.

In 1976 a State of Emergency (the second in post-Independence Jamaica, the first having been in 1966) was declared and 500 people were detained.

The People's National Party won the General Elections with 47 seats as against 13 seats for the JLP.

Cindy Breakspeare of Jamaica won the Miss World Contest in London.

In 1977, the Personal Travel Allowance was reduced to US$50 per year.

In February, the Government bought some of the mining assets in the local Kaiser Bauxite Company.

In April, Government acquired some of the assets of Reynolds Jamaica Limited at a cost of US$7.5 million.

In May the post of Ombudsman was established for the first time.

On August 6, Sir Alexander Bustamante died at the age of 94. He was the last surviving National Hero of Jamaica.

On October 18, Fidel Castro, President of Cuba paid a six-day official visit to Jamaica.

In 1978 the franchise was extended to include eighteen-year-olds by the Law Reform (Age of Majority) Act.

The Government accepted an Opposition Proposal to set up an Electoral Commission to be entrenched in due course in the Constitution. The Electoral Commission was established to deal with elections and constitutional boundaries. The Commission consists of an Independent Chairman, two Government representatives, two Opposition representatives and two other Independent members.

Mr. Vivian Blake, Q.C., P.N.P., M.P. for North-Eastern St. Ann, resigned in August 1978.

Percy Hayles who won the Commonwealth Lightweight Boxing Championship in 1968 by defeating Allotey of Ghana, in Ghana, was killed in a motor car accident on August 24.

Air Jamaica increased its revenues by 54.5%. The company's profit of $9.5 million was 9.8% of revenues.

In 1979, in December, the Jamaica Labour Party declared itself to be a Social Democratic Party.

In 1980, on March 24, the Government decided to discontinue efforts to finalize a standby agreement with the International Monetary Fund.

On April 1, the Government sought to re-schedule a national debt of US$186 million.

In May 21, a fire at the Eventide Home for the Aged, claimed the lives of 153 old women.

On June 24, a plot was discovered by the Jamaica Defence Force to overthrow the Government by force. Twenty-four JDF personnel and three civilians were detained. All those tried were eventually freed.

In July, it was estimated that there had been 223 violent deaths (at the hands of gunmen) in the first six months of 1980. Eleven members of the Security Forces were killed by gunmen and sixty-three civilians killed violently by other means.

Hurricane Allen passed by the island and did damage estimated at J$155.5 million mainly in agriculture and the tourist industry on the north coast.

In October the Jamaica Labour Party swept the polls in the General Elections, winning 51 seats as against 9 seats for the PNP. Edward Seaga was sworn in as Jamaica's fifth Prime Minister.

Rt. Hon. Edward Seaga,
Prime Minister of Jamaica,
1980 – 1989.

In 1981, in March, the Jamaica Labour Party swept the local government elections.

In April, the Governor General, Mr. Florizel Glasspole, was knighted by Queen Elizabeth on the recommendation of the Prime Minister and was designated The Most Honourable Sir Florizel Glasspole G.C.M.G., O.N.

On April 20, Robert Nesta Marley, the Reggae Superstar, was invested with the Order of Merit (O.M.).

In April, the Government negotiated an IMF loan of $698 million with positive and flexible terms.

Montego Bay was declared a city on May 1.

On May 11, Robert Nesta Marley died in Miami after a long illness.

On August 23, Jamaica was chosen as the Headquarters of the International Seabed Authority.

On October 23, Jamaica broke off diplomatic relations with Cuba.

In 1982, in February, Lady Bustamante was invested with the Order of Jamaica.

On April 7, the President of the United States of America, Mr. Ronald Reagan, and his wife, came to Jamaica on a State Visit. They departed on April 8.

On April 11, the President of Germany, Mr. Karl Carstens, visited Jamaica.

The President of Venezuela, Mr. Louis Herrerra Campin, visited Jamaica on August 2.

In 1983, on February 13, Her Majesty Queen Elizabeth II, and His Royal Highness the Duke of Edinburgh came on a visit to Jamaica.

On February 15, the Interim Headquarters of the International Seabed Authority was officially opened by Her Majesty.

A session of the International Seabed Authority being held in a conference room of the Jamaica Conference Centre.

In November, the Government announced new elections following a devaluation of the dollar from $1.78 to $3.15 to US$1. In response to an Opposition criticism of its actions and a call for the resignation of the Minister of Finance, the JLP Government on November 26 announced new General Elections to be held on December 15. The Opposition PNP countered that the Government had broken its word not to hold elections until a new electoral list was ready, and decided not to participate.

In the elections, 54 JLP candidates were returned unopposed and six others won seats contested by independents and minor parties. For the first time in Jamaica's history, all sixty seats in Parliament were held by members of the same party.

Exercises on Chapter 14

1) What were the political philosophies of the two major political parties in Jamaica during the period 1972-1983?

2) Which Party won the General Election in 1972? On what date was the election held? What was the final count in seats? Who was sworn in as Prime Minister?

3) How many PNP Senators were sworn in? On what date? How many JLP Senators were sworn in? On what date?

4) When was Parliament opened? Where? What took place that day out of the ordinary?

5) When were the Centenary celebrations of Kingston as Capital of Jamaica opened? What was the opening function and where was it held?

6) When did Prime Minister Michael Manley get married and to whom? How many Prime Ministers of Jamaica have got married while in office?

7) On what date did a Jamaican Trade Mission leave the island to visit European and Asian States? Name two Communist Countries visited.

8) Give the date of the retirement of Sir Clifford Campbell from the post of Governor-General. How long had he served? Who acted after his retirement? Who was sworn in as the new Governor-General?

9) When was Free Education announced and by whom? What does the term mean?

10) When was the bauxite levy imposed?

11) Who was the first woman to be appointed Ambassador by Jamaica? To which country was she sent?

12) What is meant by the term 'State of Emergency' and when was the last one declared in Jamaica?

13) Which party won the 1976 elections?

14) Who was Sir Alexander Bustamante? When did he die?

15) When was the post of Ombudsman first established in Jamaica?

16) What was the name of the hurricane which struck the island in 1980 and how did it affect the island?

17) Which General Election was known for the flood of political violence it brought with it?

18) Which party won the 1980 elections?

19) From which world power did Jamaica receive much financial aid?

20) Who was Robert Nesta Marley and with what title was he invested?

21) When did Jamaica break off diplomatic relations with Cuba?

22) Which three world leaders visited Jamaica in 1982?

23) When was the official opening of the Interim Headquarters of the International Seabed Authority? Who performed the official opening?

24) In which year were all sixty seats in Parliament gained by members of the same party? Name the party.

JAMAICA HISTORY PART 6: 1962–1993

CHAPTER 15

POST-INDEPENDENCE 1983 – 1993

The period 1983-1993 saw a change in the economic climate of Jamaica, as first a world recession depleted Jamaica's fortunes, especially in bauxite, and a blossoming economic stability was near-ruined by the worst hurricane in Jamaica's history, on September 12, 1988.

A change of government from the Jamaica Labour Party to the People's National Party on February 9, 1989, did not alter the economic philosophy at work, for Mr. Michael Manley declared that the PNP had embraced the free market economic system with the private sector as the engine of development. Accordingly, determined efforts were made to 'free up' the economy with the acceleration of privatization of Government hotels begun by the previous JLP Government, and the expansion of privatization to Government properties, sugar estates, and so on. The Exchange Control Act was abolished, and exchange rates were left to respond to the fluctuations of the market

In the period 1983-85, the economy was hard put to remain stable, and massive loans were sought and obtained to keep it alive. However, from 1986 to 1988 the economy strengthened with the dollar remaining stable at Ja$5.50 to US$1.

In 1986, the PNP had defeated the JLP in Local Government Elections winning 128 divisions to the JLP's 59 and taking over control of all Parish Councils except for St. Thomas. The PNP repeated its dominance in Local Government Elections in 1990 when it won 136 divisions to the JLP's 51 and kept control of all Parish Councils, again with the exception of St. Thomas.

On February 9, 1989, the PNP defeated the JLP in General Elections with its slogan 'We put people first.' The PNP won 45 seats to the JLP's 15, but with the defection of Mr. Karl Samuda from the

JLP to the PNP, the House division became 46 PNP and 14 JLP members.

In March 1992, Mr. Michael Manley resigned as Prime Minister and Leader of the PNP. He was succeeded by Mr. P. J. Patterson who defeated Miss Portia Simpson in a party run-off.

The PNP called early General Elections in 1993. Once again, the PNP defeated the JLP, this time by 52 seats to 8. Prime Minister P. J. Patterson was returned to office and retained his Leadership of the People's National Party.

**Rt. Hon. P. J. Patterson,
Prime Minister of Jamaica
since 1992**

Jamaica received much aid from the USA, Canada, UK and Europe and Japan during the period 1983 to 1993.

Sir Florizel Glasspole retired as Governor-General in 1991, after having served for eighteen years since May 1973 during both PNP and JLP Governments. He was succeeded by Howard Cooke, former PNP Minister of Education. Sir Howard and his wife, Lady Cooke, have been following in the tradition set by the late Sir Clifford Campbell and Sir Florizel Glasspole and their distinguished spouses.

The International Monetary Fund continued in the 80s and 90s to influence Jamaica's economic policy because, to get international assistance and loans, the IMF 'certificate' was obligatory.

In 1993, the Government declared that the three-year loan agreement with the IMF which demanded quarterly tests on the economy would be Jamaica's last loan from the IMF.

In 1983 Lawrence Rowe led a rebel West Indies Cricket team to play in apartheid South Africa. A Carl Stone Poll showed that 68 per cent of those tested supported the team's decision to play there.

The Jamaican dollar moved from J$1.78 to US$1, to J$3.15 to US$1 by the end of the year.

In October 1983, Jamaica and Barbados accepted the call made by Dame Eugenia Charles of Dominica to send troops to Grenada to act as police in charge of prisoners taken by the US troops. The US had invaded Grenada to seize power from Communists in the Maurice Bishop Government who had overthrown Prime Minister Bishop and then assassinated him and some of his Ministers. The rebels were keeping the Governor-General, Sir Paul Scoon, hostage in the Governor General's residence. Cubans were assisting the Grenadian Communists, and some died in the fighting following the invasion. There were no Jamaican casualties. Grenada returned to elective Governments in 1994.

The PNP under Mr. Michael Manley did not contest the elections held on December 15, and the governing JLP won all 60 seats under Prime Minister Edward Seaga. This was the shortest JLP term in Jamaica's history (1980-83).

In 1984 the *Gleaner* celebrated 150 years of publication and, with the cooperation of the Minister of Education, Dr. Mavis Gilmour, CIDA, USAID, UNESCO and thirty-three private sector companies, launched the Primary Textbook Scheme which assured all children attending primary schools of a number of textbooks free of cost. The books were printed on newsprint.

The Auditor General's Report again referred to irregularities in Government Departments.

The Hon. Edwin Allen, O.J., the Minister of Education responsible for the New Deal in Education in 1965, died at age 78 in February.

In August, the Centenary of the birth of the National Hero, Alexander Bustamante, was celebrated at several functions.

In 1985 Canasol. a new drug developed from cannabis (or ganja), was introduced by the Hon. Professor Manley West and the Hon. Dr. Albert Lockhart for the treatment of glaucoma, an eye disease. Both were awarded the Order of Merit in 1987.

A World Bank project was launched for a pilot group of All Age Schools to be upgraded and for a common curriculum for the 12 to 15 age group.

In 1986 in June there was a high toll of death and damage from flood rains.

In July the PNP won the Local Government elections.

The Anti-Litter Act of 1985 was implemented for the first time.

First degrees, Bachelor of Education were granted by the College of Arts, Science and Technology with others to be awarded in Home Economics and Engineering.

In 1987 in February the Hon. Edna Manley, O.M., widow of National Hero, the Right Excellent Norman Manley, and mother of former Prime Minister Michael Manley and of Dr. Douglas Manley died. She was given a State funeral and was buried beside her husband in the Shrine area of National Heroes' Park.

In April, flood rains caused havoc in Clarendon, St. Catherine and Portland.

The Rt. Hon. Margaret Thatcher, Prime Minister of Britain, visited Jamaica in July.

In August, Jamaica celebrated 'Jamaica 25', the 25th Anniversary of Jamaican Independence.

President Miguel de la Madrid of Mexico visited in August and President Dr. Auelt Masire of Botswana, Africa, in October.

The Centenary of the birth of National Hero Marcus Garvey was celebrated at several functions. His son Dr. Julius Garvey and Coretta Scott King, widow of famed American Civil Rights leader and Nobel prize winner Martin Luther King, visited and shared in the celebrations.

Flood rains in April killed one person and wreaked havoc in Clarendon, St. Catherine and Portland.

Over 150 AIDS cases were reported.

In 1988 The Year of the Worker was celebrated.

The PNP marked the 50th anniversary of its founding on September 18, 1938.

Dr. Julius Nyerere, former President of Tanzania, was guest speaker at a Founder's Day Banquet in June.

A heavy earthquake hit Jamaica on May 16, the strongest in 30 years.

The *Jamaica Record*, a new daily newspaper, appeared in July.

A $50 Bill with portrait of Sam Sharpe (National Hero) was issued in July.

An agreed political code of conduct was signed by the JLP and the PNP in August and Mr. Justice Kerr was appointed Ombudsman for Political Affairs.

On September 12, Hurricane Gilbert devastated Jamaica. Hundreds of houses were destroyed and agriculture was severely affected. Forty-five people died as a result of the storm. Gilbert was the first hurricane in 37 years to hit Jamaica directly. It travelled the full length of the island from Morant Point to Negril Point, with winds of up to 265 km (160 miles) per hour.

Help came to Jamaica from many countries, mobilized by the government. A one-month State of Emergency from September 14 to October 14 was observed in St.Thomas, St. Catherine, and the Corporate Area.

A Secondary and High School Book Rental Scheme was launched, with loan assistance from British Government.

The first phase of a plan to upgrade Secondary to High Schools was introduced, and some new Technical High Schools were established.

On November 11, an earthquake measuring 5.2 on the Richter Scale rocked the island.

The University Council of Jamaica Secretariat was introduced. The Council has the power to approve or to reject tertiary education programmes and degrees.

In 1989, in February, the People's National Party led by Mr. Michael Manley defeated the governing Jamaica Labour Party led by the Prime Minister Edward Seaga by 45 seats to 15. A new Cabinet took office.

Sir Florizel Glasspole, now eighty years of age, declared that in 1990 he would step down from being Governor General.

Sir Philip Sherlock, former UWI Vice Chancellor, was awarded the Order of Merit.

The new radio stations, KLAS, Irie FM and Radio Waves began broadcasting.

The dollar moved from J$5.50 to US$1 to J$6.50 to US $1.

The National Association of the Teachers of English recommended that dialect be used to support English in schools.

In 1990 "Hardships there were, but stability too" said the *Gleaner* in summarizing the year.

51% of a Carl Stone poll opposed big salary increases to Cabinet Ministers and MPs.

JLP Opposition was split by the dismissal of five MPs from the Opposition Shadow Cabinet. A Carl Stone Poll showed that 49% of the respondents opposed the dismissal.

Mr. Alistair McIntyre assumed the Vice-Chancellorship of the University of the West Indies, and Professor Leslie Robinson became Principal of the Mona Campus of the UWI.

In 1991 Nelson Mandela, the Leader of the African National Congress in South Africa, visited Jamaica in July with his wife, Winnie. The two days of their visit were "emotionally charged" as the welcome was tumultuous, perhaps the most tumultuous since the visit of Emperor Haile Selassie in 1966.

Mr. Mandela was given an honorary degree by the University of the West Indies.

Sir Florizel Glasspole, Governor General since 1973, retired and was succeeded by Sir Howard Cooke who took office on August 1.

Sir Clifford Campbell, the first native Governor General (appointed November 1962), and the second Governor General after Sir Kenneth Blackburne (who was Governor General from August 1962 to November 1962) died in September at age 90.

A General Consumption Tax was introduced replacing several taxes and duties. The rate was 10 percent of most things bought or professional services rendered. There were some exemptions, for example: petrol and basic foodstuffs.

The Most Honourable Sir Howard Cooke, Governor-General of Jamaica since 1991

In 1992 the Rt. Hon. Mr. Michael Manley, PNP Leader and Prime Minister, resigned in Mach for reasons of health. He was succeeded by the Rt. Hon. P.J. Patterson who had defeated the Hon. Portia Simpson for the succession to Mr. Manley as PNP Leader in an election conducted at the National Arena.

The *Jamaica Record* ceased publication in July, and the *Jamaica Herald* began publication in July, thus becoming the country's third daily the others being the *Daily Gleaner* and the *Star.*

Power 106, a new independent radio station, began broadcasting.

The Jamaican dollar slid to J$25 to US$1.00.

In 1993 Merlene Ottey was crowned "Queen of Athletics" on winning the gold medal at Stuttgart, Germany, in August at the World Championship Games. She was named Special Envoy by the Government.

Sugar factories were privatized, following the earlier privatization of the Marcus Garvey Building, the Wyndham Hotel, the National Commercial Bank, and several other Government properties.

Lisa Hanna became the third Jamaican to win the Miss World Beauty crown. The contest was held in South Africa.

Tourism became the top foreign exchange earner, bringing US $953 million into the economy.

Free education was replaced by cost-sharing education at the secondary level.

A new television station, CVM TV, began operating.

The *Observer* newspaper began as a weekly in late 1992.

Pope John Paul II visited Jamaica in August.

Reform of Secondary Education, R.O.S.E., began, funded by the World Bank.

LOVE FM, a religious radio station, began broadcasting.

General Elections to Parliament 1980, 1983, 1989, 1993

The following information from the Electoral office, dated March 16, 1994, is of interest. It sets out the number of voters on the list for each election, the number of votes cast, the number of votes won by the People's National Party (PNP) the Jamaica Labour Party (JLP), Independents (IND), the Christian Conscience Movement (CCM), Jamaica United Front (JUF) and the Republican Party of Jamaica (REP).

Voting Patterns 1980–1997					
		October 1980	December 1983	February 1989	March 1993
1	Voters on list	990,427	990,586	1,078,760	1,002,571
2	Votes cast	860,746	26,543	845,485	669,164
3	Percent of voters on list who voted	86.9	2.68	78.37	66.74
4	**Votes**				
	PNP	350,064 [40.66%]	Did not take part	473,754 (56%)	401,746 (60%)
	JLP	502,115 (58.33%)	23,363 (88%)	362,389 (42.86%)	263,472 (39.37%)
	IND	527	1,587	628	3,833
	CCM	No part	704	No part	No part
	J.U.F.	No part	144	No part	No part
	R.E.P.	No part	No part	No part	133
5	Seats - JLP	51	60	15	8
	PNP	9	No part	45	52

Exercises on Chapter 15

1) Was there a difference in the politico-economic philosophy of the two major parties during 1983-1993?

2) When were Jamaican armed forces sent to Grenada and why?

3) When did Hurricane Gilbert hit Jamaica?

4) Did the dollar remain stable in the period? If not, describe the devaluation.

5) Who were the Prime Ministers in this period?

6) When did Nelson Mandela visit Jamaica?

7) When did Margaret Thatcher visit Jamaica?

8) When did Pope John Paul II visit Jamaica?

9) Who became Miss World in 1993?

10) Name the first athlete to be named a Special Envoy for Jamaica, and give the reason.

11) Name the parties other than the PNP and JLP that took part in elections in 1980, 1983, 1989 and 1993.

12) Describe the development of the privatization programme in the period.

13) What educational innovations were there?

14) Which parties won the elections in 1983, 1989 and 1993?